Can Homophobia Be Cured?

CAN HOMOPHOBIA BE CURED?

*Wrestling with Questions
That Challenge the Church*

BRUCE HILTON

Abingdon Press
Nashville

CAN HOMOPHOBIA BE CURED?
WRESTLING WITH QUESTIONS THAT CHALLENGE THE CHURCH

Copyright © 1992 by Abingdon Press

93 94 95 96 97 98 99 00 01 02 03—10 9 8 7 6 5 4 3

This book is printed on recycled, acid-free paper.

Library of Congress Cataloging-in-Publication Data

HILTON, BRUCE.
    Can Homophobia be cured? : wrestling with questions that challenge the church / Bruce Hilton.
        p. cm.
    Includes bibliographical references.
    ISBN 0-687-04631-9 (alk. paper)
    1. Homosexuality—Religious aspects—Christianity. 2. Gays. 3. Homosexuality—Biblical teaching. 4. Church work with gays.
I. Title.
BR115.H6H54   1992
261.8'35766—dc20
                                                        92-8588
                                                        CIP

Scripture quotations, unless otherwise noted, are from the New Revised Standard Version of the Bible, copyright 1989 by the Division of Christian Education of the National Council of the Churches of Christ in the USA. Used by permission.

Quotations from Robert A. Bernstein on pages 28, 113-14 are from "My Daughter Is a Lesbian," *The New York Times*, February 24, 1988. Copyright © 1988 by The New York Times Company. Reprinted by permission.

MANUFACTURED IN THE UNITED STATES OF AMERICA

This book is dedicated to
Steve,
Phil,
Tom,
and Paul,
with sincere appreciation
for all they have taught the old man.

Acknowledgments

I'm deeply grateful to:

Virginia Young Hilton, companion in this learning journey, for wisdom, encouragement, patience, and joy.

Jim and Warren, faithful friends.

Ellie and Jean, Connie and Judy, Mary and Judy, Rick, Morris, . . . and many others, gay and straight, whose need to be anonymous is one of the terrible costs of homophobia.

Contents

Where there is hatred, let me sow love.

Prayer of St. Francis

A Mother Writes

A mother writes, nine years after her son's death:

To all the Bobbys and Janes out there, I say these words to you, as I would to my own precious children:

Please don't give up hope in life, or in yourselves. You are very special to me, and I am working very hard to help make this life a better and safer place for you to live in.

I firmly believe—though I did not, back then—that my son Bobby's suicide was the end result of homophobia and ignorance within most Protestant and Catholic churches, and consequently within society, our public schools, our own family.

Bobby was not a drunk, nor did he use drugs. It's just that we could never accept him for who he was—a gay person.

We hoped God would heal him of being gay. According to God's word, as we were led to understand it, Bobby had to repent or God would damn him to hell and eternal punishment.

That I ever accepted—*believed*—such depravity of God toward my son or any human being has caused me much remorse and shame.

What a travesty of God's love, for children to grow up believing themselves to be evil, with only a slight inclination toward goodness, and that they will remain undeserving of God's love from birth to death.

Looking back, I realize how depraved it was to instill false guilt in an innocent child's conscience, causing a distorted image of life, God, and self; leaving little if any feeling of personal worth.

Had I viewed my son's life with a pure heart, I would have recognized him as a tender spirit in God's eyes.

I would have seen a life that, for the most part, parallels the heterosexual life: being; learning; working; loving and caring for another human being; having someone to grow old with, someone to share the joys and sorrows of life with, someone to share God's wonderful world with.

We never thought of a gay person as an equal, a lovable and valuable part of God's creation. What a travesty of God's unconditional love!

Is it any wonder our young people give up on love, as Bobby did, and the hope of ever receiving the validation they deserve as beautiful human beings?

Is it any wonder suicide statistics are increasing among young people, and even more so among young gays and lesbians?

Bobby dropped out of high school in April 1981, two months before his graduation.

With the right help to fight the homophobia surrounding him, he might have found the hope and encouragement he needed to finish school.

As a result of my son's death, I have joined other caring people to try to make a pathway with knowledge and understanding within our public school system, a pathway that in time may be traveled with dignity and freedom from fear, for gay and lesbian students, and any student who is subjected to discrimination.

Promise me you will keep trying.

As Tina Turner says in her song, "Love and compassion, their day is coming; all else are castles built in the air."

Bobby gave up on love. I hope you won't. You are always in my thoughts.

With love,

Mary Griffith
Walnut Creek, California

Chapter One

Asking the
Right Question

ho'mo-pho'bi-a *n*. irrational fear or hatred of homosexual people.

An ugly word; nobody likes it. The disease itself is pretty ugly too. I've had a case of it since I was a little kid. Chances are, you have too.

It is so universal, and so taken for granted, that most of us aren't aware of its presence in us. It's like water to a fish—the last thing we'd notice.

Unlike sexual orientation, homophobia is contagious. Children can catch it from an adult; in fact, that's the main mode of transmission.

Its effects range from mild distaste to homicidal rage, from judgmental attitudes to obsession.

In its more virulent stages, it causes at least 100 people to commit murder in the United States each year, and maybe 1,000 others to attack fellow humans—simply because the victims are homosexual—severely enough to put them in the hospital.

The Houston police department didn't believe that sort of thing went on, despite repeated requests by the gay and lesbian community for better protection. Finally, in August of 1991, the department agreed to send out decoys—male officers in civilian clothes, walking in pairs—to the areas of alleged danger.

In the first week, four of the decoy officers were attacked. Two were tear-gassed, and two were beaten with a baseball bat. In that first week a dozen people were arrested in attempted assaults.

In a classic understatement, a police spokesman told the press, "We certainly have been made more aware of the problems faced by the gay community."

But most effects of homophobia are not that immediate or spectacular. Young homosexual people, struggling with sexual feelings they know are at odds with the culture around them, grow up with feelings of desperation, rejection, and low self-esteem that they often don't dare express, even to their families. Secretly aware of feelings they may have had as long as they can remember, they hear all around them, every day, jokes and slurs and comments that make it clear those feelings are not "normal." Many of them, like victims of racial and other bigotries, come to believe the casual vilification that fills the air.

No wonder many gay people struggle with abuse of alcohol and other drugs. No wonder a recent federal study found that suicide among gay teens was two to three times as frequent as among other teens.

> Dear Beth,
> I am having panic attacks every night, and I can't ever get to sleep. I'm so tired I can't think. It's all because of this BIG problem. I'm gay. I've known it since I was 11, and I can't stand lying about it anymore. But how can I tell the people who adopted me and have nurtured me for years? They would never be able to accept it because they are VERY traditional. All I can think to do is kill myself, but I'm too chicken even to do that.
>
> *—Letter to "Ask Beth,"*
> *syndicated advice columnist for teenagers*

Having a gay or lesbian child can be a threat to a family. In some families with a homosexual child, homophobia can cause parents to abandon the traditional family values of love and trust, rejecting their own children. Others, like Mary Griffith, waste time and energy trying to "cure" their children, sending them continual messages of disappointment, disapproval, and conditional love.

> "I'd feel like killing them. They probably wouldn't be allowed in my house again. I'd completely reject them."
>
> —*36-year-old San Diego man,*
> *asked by a reporter how he would feel about*
> *having gay children*

Though less important than our estrangement from one another, there's another, more clearly defined cost of homophobia: business and taxpayer dollars. One of the clearest examples comes from the armed forces: Despite two Pentagon studies that show that gay men and lesbians are as good or better at their military jobs than heterosexual enlisted personnel, the armed forces have spent $251 million since 1973 tracking down and expelling enlisted gay men and lesbians.

> When I was in the military they gave me a medal for killing two men—and a discharge for loving one.
>
> —*Epitaph of former Air Force*
> *Sgt. Leonard Matlovich*

But the highest cost, the greatest damage done by homophobia may have been to—and by—the Church.

Influenced heavily by the society around us, we've worried ourselves sick over why some men fall in love with men, and some women love women. We've thrown up ramparts, both mental and bureaucratic, to

19

make sure such people get the message: You are not welcome.

We've been obsessed with this issue, which the Gospel writers apparently thought to be of such low priority that they include no sayings of Jesus about it—if, indeed, he mentioned it at all.

And in so doing, we've wallowed in self-righteousness—the sin that Jesus seems to have taken most seriously and mentioned most often.

The tragic result is that a Family of people brought together by the Sovereign of Love has become an exclusive institution, intent on keeping the "wrong" people out. A Book whose central message is "love thy neighbor" is used as a key to lock out people our society tells us to fear.

Rather than being transformed by the renewing of our minds, we of the Church have become conformed to this world.

"Because I finally found the courage and strength I needed to drop my mask, the church that I grew up in has rejected me. Where I once was allowed to serve, I am no longer permitted. They are unable to fathom any other possibility other than I am lost in sin. They will not accept the testimony of those who have experienced what it is to be gay. They would rather listen to those who have no experience, only armchair theories— because then they do not have to think, or change, or risk, or hurt."

—Arthur L. McBride,
Nashville, Tennessee

"They tie up heavy burdens, hard to bear, and lay them on the shoulders of others; but they themselves are unwilling to lift a finger to move them."
—Matthew 23:4

This book is for people who sense there must be more, in the silence that surrounds this subject, than we have been told. It asks questions that we often forget to ask. I don't expect you to agree with all my answers. But if it makes you wonder about the hidden messages of a homophobic society, then it will have been worthwhile for both of us.

Among all the questions, however, there is just one that counts.

Overwhelmed by the nearly universal bigotry of society, we of the Church have forgotten that the *primary* issue is not the causes of homosexuality, or whether it can be "cured," or whether its practice is a sin, but *do we love our neighbors, whoever they are?*

In this book we'll take up other questions. We'll look at aspects of sexuality and the faith that you may not have heard in church. But those are not the central questions.

The key question is one that only you can answer:

Regardless of how I feel about the orientation and practices of homosexual people, do I love them, and am I willing to work toward making my congregation a place where they feel love?

Now I happen to be a United Methodist, so this book will contain more references and citations from a United Methodist context than from any other one context. You can be sure, however, that even if you are not a United Methodist, most of these questions—or variations on them—are being asked by members of your own church as well.

The Social Principles of The United Methodist Church state:

Homosexuals no less than heterosexuals are persons of sacred worth, who need the ministry and guidance of

21

the church in their struggles for human fulfillment, as well as the spiritual and emotional care of a fellowship which enables reconciling relationships with God, with others and with self.

And in the Scriptures:

Those who say, "I love God," and hate their brothers or sisters, are liars; for those who do not love a brother or sister whom they have seen, cannot love God whom they have not seen. The commandment we have from him is this: those who love God must love their brothers and sisters also.

—I John 4:20-21

Chapter Two

A Question
About Feelings

"[Students who are openly gay] are teased to death. They are either hit or called names. Some kids have threatened to beat them up in the locker room. They are constantly teased and ostracized.

"Until we start dealing with that issue the way we deal with racism, nothing is going to happen. We all need to be a lot more vocal about what is going on, but today 'faggot' is the biggest putdown kids can think of."

—High school counselor, quoted in Denver Post.

"I don't like it when my friends put down gay people. But telling them to stop would be social suicide."

—13-year-old heterosexual boy, quoted in Open Hands.

*   *   *

QUESTION: Where Do Our Strong Feelings
About Homosexuality
Come From?

Feelings of ridicule, contempt, and disgust toward gay people are widespread, but that doesn't mean that these feelings are normal.

We do learn them so early, and they're so common, that we hardly know we have them—much less think about questioning them.

One way we know we're not *born* disliking gay people is that attitudes toward them vary so widely from one culture to the other. As far as we can tell, every place and every time has had some people who were romantically and erotically attracted to their own sex. In some cultures, that has been a hanging offense. (In England, the first anti-gay law was passed in 1553; the first person hanged was Bishop John Atherton). At the opposite extreme, some Native American tribes honored these *berdache* as especially wise and sought their advice on important decisions.

In the first ten centuries after Christ, few if any European states had laws about what we call homosexual acts (the word *homosexual* wasn't coined until late in the nineteenth century). The artist who painted *The Last Supper* and the English king who authorized the Bible translation named after him made no secret of their homophilic orientation. Much of the time it was "live and let live."

The fact that there have always been same-sex lovers isn't necessarily an argument for accepting or rejecting them. It's cited here as a reminder that attitudes toward them have always been determined by the *culture*. Babies are not born hating or fearing gay people; they grow up learning from the people around them to hate or fear.

Here are some of the reasons why most of us grow up feeling uncomfortable about gay people.

1. What People Around Us Say

Kids pick up their parents' silences, their reluctance to talk about certain topics. They pick up the judgmental attitude in a chance remark. They learn, from rude jokes and crude remarks, just who they're expected to respect and who they're not.

In school, long before we have any idea what *lesbian, gay,* or *homosexual* mean, we learn that homosexual people are fair game for ridicule. (Remember in grade school, somebody laughingly being accused of being "a homo" because he was wearing green or orange on a Thursday—Queer Day?)

While racism and sexism still infest our national psyche, it has at least become unfashionable for public figures to express those sentiments openly. But gay people are still fair game. Some members of Congress have built careers on verbal gay-bashing.

Only recently have we begun to see leaders stand up and question homophobia in the same way they have been questioning and challenging for years when the subject was racism or sexism.

The number 1 reason we have feelings of fear, disgust, contempt, or hate toward gay people as a group is that we have been taught to do so by the words and actions of those around us.

> In one of the most alarming findings, the report found that while teenagers surveyed were reluctant to advocate open bias against racial and ethnic groups, they were emphatic about disliking homosexual men and women. They are perceived "as legitimate targets that can be openly attacked," the report said. . . . The feelings were as strong among 12-year-olds as among 17-year-olds. Many students added gratuitous vicious comments about homosexuals; that was not the case with other groups.
>
> New York Times *on the report*
> *by the New York Governor's Task Force on*
> *Bias-Related Violence*

25

2. Our Instinctive Bias Against Anybody Who Varies from the "Norm"

If there is anything inborn about homophobia, it's the human tendency to shrink from anything "different." This is especially true in our growing years, while we're trying to sort out our own selfhood and place in the world.

Homophobia isn't the only example of this, of course. It's been with us since the people of one cave worried about the people in the cave across the valley. Humorist Garrison Keillor, in his book, *How to Talk Minnesotan,* suggests two essential phrases if you're traveling in the Land of Lakes: "You bet," if you like something, and "That's different," if you disapprove. You don't have to be from Minnesota (as I am) to have it drilled into your subconscious that what's "different" is often unacceptable.

That's why we have put-down words like:

> misfit
> pervert
> abnormal
> queer
> freak
> unnatural

"Another thing the Elders liked about Earthlings was that they feared and hated other Earthlings who did not look and talk exactly as they did. They made life a hell for each other as well as for what they called 'lower animals.' They actually thought of strangers as lower animals. . . .

"The Elders made us think that the Creator on the big throne hated strangers as much as we did, and that we would be doing Him a big favor if we tried to exterminate them by any and all means possible."

Description of a science fiction story by a character in Kurt Vonnegut's novel Hocus Pocus

3. The Fact That the Information We Get About Gay People Is Selective— and Mostly Negative

It's the negative things that make news. We see head-lines about "homosexual killers" and "gay molesters." But if we want to be fair and honest about this, we'll note three important things that are going on:

a. Straights who do the same awful things are not identified by sexual orientation. The headlines never say "straight man kills 10," or "heterosexual molests child." It's the way we usually think and talk—using an adjective with what we consider unusual, but not with what we consider the norm. (We do this with gender, too: There are "doctors" and "women doctors," "preachers" and "women preachers.")

This language not only *reflects* our attitudes, but *reinforces* them. We end up with "information" that is completely wrong. The United States Department of Health, Education, and Welfare says, for example, that 90 percent of all sexual child abuse in this country is committed by heterosexual men on minor females (*Child Abuse and Neglect: The Problem and Its Management*, HEW 75-30073). Any social service worker, police officer, or therapist will tell you the same. The vast majority of murderers, serial or otherwise, are heterosexual.

b. Misusing God's gift of sexuality to exploit others is wrong, whoever does it. This includes those who abuse children or partners, harass those in their power, or denigrate the gift by casual use—regardless of whether they're heterosexual, homosexual, or bisexual.

c. Stereotyping blinds us to the fact that most gay people never make the headlines and don't fit the images many of us cling to. We mistake the exception for the usual. This will continue to be true as long as

27

homophobia forces the large majority of gay people to hide their orientation.

> The much maligned "life-style" of the average homosexual person is about as lurid as our own, centered on such mundane matters as jobs, friends, hobbies, and church. The gay community, it turns out, contains about the same proportion of saints to rascals as any other.

> —*Robert A. Bernstein,*
> *retired Justice Department lawyer and father of a lesbian woman,*
> *in an Op-Ed article for the* New York Times

4. Sexism

The devaluing of women is still one of the strongest strains of Western thought, despite our sporadic attempts to make things more just. Buried deep in the subconscious of most of us—men and women—is the belief that women ought to fill different, subservient, less important roles than men. There are symptoms of this all around us; in the church, they range from the continuing battles over ordaining women to the panic and rage caused in some quarters when we address God as anything other than male.

So it shouldn't be any surprise that for many men, the most objectionable aspect of male homosexuality is that one of the men might—but not necessarily—assume a "female" role. A *man*, deliberately lowering himself, acting like a *woman!* Nor should it be any surprise that, by and large, fathers are more threatened by the idea of having a gay male child than mothers are. The stereotype of an effeminate male or—even worse, a man acting as the passive (female) partner in a sex act—is enough to raise the blood pressure of any red-blooded, football-loving, gun-toting, muscle-flexing heterosexual American man.

In fact, the stereotype of all gay men as effeminate is no more accurate than the stereotype, in the previous sentence, of heterosexual men. But, as a gay man said to me, "We have to work for justice for women, because as long as people hate and fear what is female, they'll hate and fear the female in me."

5. The Tendency to Genitalize Our Thinking About Homosexuality

A group of fundamentalist protesters at San Francisco's Gay Freedom Day parade summed up this view pretty well with their sign: Sodomites Repent.

If we can take all the complexity of a loving relationship between two people and think of it as no more than the joining of a couple of organs, it's a lot easier to condemn. It lets us talk about *parts*, not people. It lets us talk about a single act, not a relationship. It distorts and trivializes the relationships and ignores realities like commitment, loyalty, and tenderness. If you're a heterosexual person, would you want your whole being summed up this way? "A heterosexual? That's somebody who indulges in penile-vaginal intercourse."

6. The Words We Use

This tendency to see gay people only in terms of what they may do in bed, interested only in sex and defined only by sex, is one reason many lesbians and gay men object to the word "homo*sexual*." None of the terms we use are universally acceptable, although *lesbians and gay men* is the phrase people of same-sex orientation use most often in their own writings. *Gay people* runs a close second. In any event, varying the phrases helps avoid a narrow stereotype, and *gay* has the advantage of having been selected by the homophilial community itself, without having had—originally, at least—a negative or pejorative taint to it.

Occasional use of *homophilia* (*love* for people of one's own sex) in place of *homosexuality* would show an awareness, at least, of the power of words.

Other phrases used to put down gay people, either unconsciously or with subtle intent: *lifestyle,* which strongly implies choice, and suggests all gay people act alike, and *sexual preference,* which also implies free choice. In view of the growing body of scientific evidence that the gender of the object of one's sexual attraction is not chosen, *sexual orientation* is probably more accurate.

By the way, the ugly slur *faggot* literally means a bundle of sticks tied together—as for a torch—and comes from the practice in the late Middle Ages of burning at the stake people accused of same-sex acts.

7. The Need for Simple Answers
When Everything Around Us Is Changing

This includes clear boundaries, unambiguous principles, and, sometimes, a scapegoat or devil to hate.

The response of the Hebrew people to drastic change is clear in the first five books of the Hebrew Scriptures. Rigid boundaries are spelled out, separating moral from immoral, Jew from foreigner, milk from meat, one kind of fabric from another, male from female. For a man to lie with a man threatened the reassuring barrier between male and female, as surely as the equally objectionable mixing of meat and milk.

Historians tell us that social upheaval put an end to the general feeling of tolerance in twelfth-century Europe; by the fourteenth century hatred and persecution of Muslims, Jews, heretics, usurers, and "sodo-mites" was the rule, not the exception.

At the same time, governments were playing on this need, using hatred of a "separate" group, a common enemy, to unify the people. The outcast group served as a sign of corruption or of moral decline, and killing or ostracizing them became an act for the good of all.

In the twentieth century, the time of greatest change known to history, the same thing has happened. As change accelerates, it's no wonder that the more rigid fundamentalist churches are thriving, and the talk-show host with the most United States radio stations specializes in flat-out pronouncements of time-proven right-wing clichés. People want clear answers, not shades of gray—and when there are no clear answers, they'll listen to somebody who claims to know.

Among the main targets of those who pander to the craving for absolutes are gay men and lesbians.

> In periods of cultural insecurity, when there are fears of regression and degeneration, the longing for strict border controls around the definition of gender, as well as race, class and nationality, becomes especially intense.
>
> —*Elaine Showalter,*
> Sexual Anarchy

8. The Ease of Talking About an Abstract Issue, Rather Than About Real People

It's always easier to misunderstand or condemn an "it" than a "he" or "she." Because of the secrecy enforced by homophobia, most gay people are still in

31

the closet; many straight people aren't aware that they know any of them. Bigotry, always harder face-to-face, thrives on anonymity:

> "I fear that for some in our church this has become a 'cheap' issue: one over which people who need not deal directly with homosexuals themselves, can get very emotional and about which they can feel very self-righteous, without any real cost to themselves."
>
> —*Bishop Marvin Stuart,*
> *in a letter to* The United Methodist Reporter

9. Our Difficulty in Dealing with Sexuality in General

The Social Principles may call sex "God's good gift to all persons," and state that all people are "fully human only when that gift is acknowledged and affirmed by themselves, the church, and society."

But we don't act as though we really believe that.

Unlike other good gifts of God, this one rarely gets discussed in Sunday school. We don't hear many sermons praising God for giving us sex. Not many hymns, either. In theory, sex is God's gift; in practice, we associate it more with the devil. We're embarrassed to talk about it except in jokes; we associate it more with sin than with grace.

In the history of our faith, it wasn't always that way. The ancient Jews weren't nearly so ambivalent. The Hebrew scriptures and the Talmud resoundingly affirm our sexual natures. In fact, other than in the code for priests in Leviticus, there's little condemnation of heterosexual intercourse in any kind of relationship, except when the woman was the property of another man.

The early Christian church didn't depart drastically from this approach. Paul, of course, was a little more grudging in his thanks for the gift of sex: "It is well for a man not to touch a woman" (I Corinthians 7:1) and, "To the unmarried and the widows I say that it is well for them to remain unmarried as I am. But . . . it is better to marry than to be aflame with passion" (I Corinthians 7:8, 9). But by and large, the church's earliest writings, including the New Testament, didn't seem to be interested in a sexual ethic. If Jesus mentioned it, the Gospel writers didn't think it was important enough to report.

But over the first three centuries, while the church was developing détente with the Roman Empire, a supreme irony was developing: The church was absorbing the sexual ideals of the conquerors' religion—rigid sexual rules and a hatred of the body.

The Romans had latched onto an old idea of the Greeks and the Zoroastrians: The body and mind are in competition. Mind is good, body is bad. Thinking is good, passion is bad. Man (rational) is good, woman (emotional) is bad. Abstinence is good, giving in to sexual feelings is bad.

The ascetics saw the body as something to be forced into submission, a hostile entity to be controlled. The philosopher Seneca believed that life's highest goal was a passionless state, in which there was nothing about which one got excited or disturbed.

Two things happened to the church in those early centuries. An emperor became Christian, and the church became the official religion; deprived of Roman idolatry as the major evil against which to fight, the church seized on sexual "purity" as its symbol of identity. Second, it made the pagan dualism, the contempt for the body, its own.

> Christianity did not make the world ascetic; rather, the
> world in which Christianity found itself strove to make
> Christianity ascetic.
>
> —*Morton Scott Enslin*, The Ethics of Paul

St. Augustine gave up his mistress after he was converted to Christianity—not because they were engaging in sex outside of marriage, but because he believed sexual intercourse itself was incompatible with the Christian life. (He defended the Hebrew fathers' polygamy, on the basis that they used their many wives for getting babies, not for pleasure.)

Since then we've come a long way in appreciating our bodies as essential to our selves, but the scent of the old ideas lingers in the air.

Most of us are unaware of the source of the ideas; they seem always to have been around: Marriage is for procreation, not pleasure. The clergy should be celibate. Sex is not discussed in polite society, and sexual feelings are not something to value—at least not in the Christian context. For that matter, we mustn't give ourselves over too much to any kind of pleasure. Women have their place, but as bodies, not minds—as mothers, not leaders.

We haven't come that far from the reaction in 1899, after Dr. Denslow Lewis addressed the American Medical Association on "The Gynecological Consideration of the Sexual Act." As a typical critic said, the subject "is attended with more or less filth and we besmirch ourselves by discussing it in public."

Given all this ambivalence, going back sixteen centuries, it's no wonder we have trouble dealing with an even more ambiguous aspect of sexuality: same-sex love.

Chapter Three

What Do We Know
About Gay People?

Virginia and I had gone to a restaurant specializing in pancakes on a Sunday morning to escape the tension at General Conference and indulge my taste for potato pancakes. It was after the breakfast rush, and the waitress, an efficient and pleasant woman in her early thirties, had time to stop and chat.

After we'd talked about the weather and the General Conference—she'd seen something about it on TV—she asked, casually, "What do the buttons stand for?"

Right at that moment of relaxation and escape, we didn't feel much like answering, because we weren't up for still another long discussion of the kind we'd been having all week.

The buttons, with a pink triangle in the middle, identified us as friends of Affirmation, the caucus of gay, lesbian, and bisexual United Methodists. For days we'd done little else than share their pain and frustration as General Conference worked on making them unwelcome in the church and engage in long, disheartening discussions with unsympathetic straights.

I wasn't up for more hostility, so I weaseled: "It's just one of the caucuses over at the conference."

She nodded and went to bring us more coffee. But later, as she stood at the cash register ringing up our bill, she suddenly looked me in the eye and said, "I want you to know, we really appreciate what you're trying to do for us over there."

I don't remember what I said, but I remember I could hardly see as I went out the door. I was thinking, "How many?"

How many gentle, rejected, *invisible* people are looking on from outside the circle we have drawn? How many times a day are they hurt by our casual remarks, our indifference, our cowardice?

* * *

QUESTION: Who Are the Homosexual People, Anyway?

Not an easy question to answer. Let's start with definitions.

The word *homosexual* gets its prefix from the Greek *homo,* meaning "the same." Professor John Money of Johns Hopkins University Medical School, co-founder of the Gender Identity Clinic there, says homosexual people have "erotic response to individuals with the same kind of sexual anatomy as oneself. It may or may not include overt homosexual behavior and physical contact."

Psychiatrist Richard Isay suggests this definition: "One whose erotic fantasy life is predominantly homosexual."

That's a start, but the problem with definitions—and the reason there are dozens of them—is that there is no way to put people into neat compartments. Especially when it comes to sexuality.

One of the most important findings in the research by Dr. Alfred Kinsey was that we can't be put in separate pigeonholes marked "gay person" or "straight person."

His team found that all of us range along a seven-point scale from exclusively heterosexual (Category 0), no same-sex fantasies or sex acts, to homosexual (Category 6), no other-sex fantasies or sex acts.

Most of us, they found, range between the two poles. Many of us fall into Kinsey's Category 1: mostly heterosexual, with only incidental same-sex thoughts or experiences. Those in Category 2 are mostly heterosexual but have had "more than incidental" same-sex thoughts or experiences.

Category 3, in the middle of the scale, is for people equally attracted to their own and to the other sex.

In Category 4 are people whose attraction is mostly to their own sex, but have had significant other-sex fantasies and experiences. And Category 5 includes those whose feelings are mostly toward the same sex, but have had only incidental feelings or experiences with the other sex.

You can see why it's so hard to define *homosexual person*. In this book, I'm using *gay, lesbian,* or *homosexual* mostly for those who consider themselves in Categories 5 and 6—those who fall in love almost exclusively or exclusively with people of the same sex. I'm using *heterosexual* or *straight* for the two categories at the other end of the scale. (I realize that *straight* at times has been used as a put-down of gay people, implying non-straights are somehow bent. But it has wide use in both the the gay and heterosexual communities, and is clearer and less awkward than the alternatives. I hope its use won't offend anyone.)

*   *   *

QUESTION: Who Are the Bisexual People?

Those in Categories 3, 4, and 5, with at least incidental fantasies and experience with both sexes, are likely
to think of themselves as bisexual. They're even harder
to identify than the people at either end of the scale,
simply because they feel prejudice from both those
groups. Some conservatives accept the idea of monogamous, committed same-sex couples, but are troubled
by self-avowed bisexual people, because *acting* on this
orientation would by definition involve multiple partners and unfaithfulness to one partner. Many lesbians
and gay men, meanwhile, consider bisexual people as
dabblers in same-sex practice, thrill-seekers, or traitors
to the gay community, who can always retreat back to
the safety of the straight world.

If you take some version of the Kinsey scale seriously, however, you realize that there are a great many
people who have the ability to fall in love with either
sex. Anthropologists report that the people of vast
regions of the world engage in bisexual activity, with
the consent of their societies; these include many
South Pacific cultures.

* * *

QUESTION: Just How Many Lesbians, Gay Men, and Bisexuals Are There?

Although Kinsey's estimate is more than forty years
out of date, it's still the only one we have. His team
found that in his sample, 4 percent of the males were
"exclusively homosexual" (Category 6) and another 8
to 15 percent "predominantly" homosexual (Categories
4 and 5).

Dr. Paul Gebhart, Kinsey's successor at the Institute for Sex Research, added newer data and used newer statistical methods to come up with the figure of 9.13 percent of men and women who have had "extensive" or "more than incidental" homosexual experience and feelings.

In homosexuality, he said, "one is talking about something which involves millions, not thousands, of U.S. citizens, and homosexuality is a phenomenon which, with only slight variation, appears to cross all geographic, ethnic, and socio-economic barriers in this country."

Some researchers believe the figures might be higher in the 1990s, since the pressures against revealing a same-sex orientation—even in private to a researcher—were much greater than they are now. (The power of such pressure is shown by the fact that China, Romania, and the Soviet Union—where repression and imprisonment of homosexual people was both the law and the party line—denied for many years that they had any gay people at all.)

If the figures are close, we're talking about a conservative estimate of 25 million people in the United States alone.

Estimating how many gay people are in the church is more difficult, because so many lesbians and gay men have read the "not welcome" signs and left. Nine percent in the United Methodist Church would be around 720,000; allowing for divorces and families with more than one gay child, you can add at least a million parents also affected by the church's attitudes.

(The exodus of gay people and their families is one hypothesis never mentioned in church publications when discussing the declining membership of denominations. The exodus of gay men and parents alone

39

could account for much of the United Methodist losses in the years since the church took an officially anti-gay stand. Of course, there are no more data for this idea than for any of the other hypotheses—including the one that "discussing homosexuality will drive people from the church.")

*   *   *

QUESTION: Why Is It So Hard to Get Accurate Data?

Even in these days of sophisticated social research, the figures are soft. Here are three of the reasons—some obvious, and some not so obvious:

1. *Most gay people are still in the closet.* As long as parents, church, and society are disapproving, and as long as there is discrimination in jobs, housing, and public safety, most lesbians and gay men are likely to hide their orientation. The number who are "out"—known to family and co-workers—may be as few as 10 percent of the whole homophilial population. In the ordained ministry, of course, those who come out are only a tiny fraction, because it means loss of one's calling and career.

2. *Most social scientists won't touch the subject.* A task force of the American Sociological Association surveyed heads of sociology departments across the country, asking whether a researcher in their department would be able to study homophilia as a subject. The answer, almost unanimously, was no.

Asked why, they said researchers feared being thought of as homosexual if they took too much interest in the subject. And even if someone were interested, getting grants to study the topic was considered unlikely.

3. *Definitions differ.* Which population will you—or can you—count? Do you count those who *say* they are lesbians or gay men? Those who engage in same-sex acts? Those who are oriented to their own sex but are celibate?

Will you include men arrested in parks looking for same-sex encounters, the overwhelming majority of whom are married and identify themselves as predominantly straight? Will you include those who engage in same-sex practices while in prison or aboard ship, but are strictly heterosexual at all other times?

The desire for numbers probably comes from our tendency to categorize and pigeonhole people; when discrimination is less, we may care less about these numbers.

* * *

QUESTION: What Causes Homosexuality?

Scientists say they don't really know how sexual orientation is determined—either same-sex or other-sex. More than a hundred theories have been suggested—including a Turkish study in 1979 that blamed homosexuality on disco music. But no single theory fits all the evidence or holds up under the rigors of peer review by other researchers.

No single hypothesis can explain why one person's romantic daydreams center on the opposite sex, while another's focus on the same sex.

This doesn't mean scientists are no help at all. They do generally agree that:

41

1. The causes of sexual orientation are probably multiple, involving many interacting factors.

2. "Nature-versus-nurture" arguments are no help, since it is likely that both biology and environment are involved.

3. Whatever the cause, sexual orientation is fixed early, and unlikely to change.

The most common theory for years was that a dominant mother and a weak father were to blame for homosexual orientation. But three researchers at the Kinsey Institute, after studying 1,300 heterosexual and homosexual men and women, concluded that "the connection between boys' relationships with their mothers and whether they become homosexual or heterosexual is hardly worth mentioning."

They also were able to rule out other family causes, including birth order, the quality of the parents' marriage, having all sisters or all brohers, and the nature of the relationship with siblings.

They found only one family difference. Gay men were less likely than heterosexual men to have had good relationships with their fathers. However, many of the gay men said they had been called "sissies" by other kids, and had had feminine interests—leading the researchers to think this may have caused fathers to feel uncomfortable with their sons. The team concluded that the fathers' reactions didn't cause the orientation, but it may have been the other way around.

Some relatively new studies strengthen the hypothesis that biology plays a part in determining sexual orientation:

The hypothalamus: In 1991, a Salk Institute researcher found small but significant differences between the brains of gay men and heterosexual men. The hypothalamus, a part of the brain associated with sexual behavior, was smaller in the gay men, and more like the hypothalamus of women than the heterosexual men's were.

The findings were very tentative, but echoed research reported three years earlier by a Dutch scientist, D.F. Swaab. He found that certain nuclei in the hypothalamus were smaller in the gay men he studied than in the heterosexual men.

The twins: A few months later, researchers at Northwestern University and Boston University said they believed heredity plays a role in sexual orientation.

They had studied 167 gay men, each of whom had either a twin brother or an adopted brother.

The study showed that of the men with an identical twin, 52 percent of the other twins were also gay. Of the men with a fraternal twin—coming from a different fertilized egg—22 percent of the other twins were gay.

Of the subjects with adopted brothers, 11 percent of the other brothers were gay.

Since each pair of brothers had been reared together, they had similar environments; "nurture" was less likely to have been a major factor in the differences between groups.

Hormones are another possible influence on the fetus. In lab animals, they have affected not only the development of the genitals, but also the sex to which the animal is attracted.

Dr. Money of Johns Hopkins suggests that our orientation is subject to strong influences during two crucial periods. One is early in pregnancy, when genes and hormones do their work. The other is soon after birth, when the family and environment do their imprinting. Either or both may be a factor, Dr. Money says.

Orientation is a vague word. When you think in terms of romantic fantasy—the generally accepted definition—it is easier to see what the scientists are telling us.

Do you remember the first romantic feelings you had as a child or early youth? The earliest I remember was when I was seven; I dreamed about Shirley Temple after seeing her in *Heidi*. Since then, my romantic fantasies and erotic feelings have been about females. I don't know why, and as of this writing, no scientist can tell me why.

I know a man who also remembers his first romantic feelings, at the age of six or seven. They were for Charles Atlas, the multi-muscled body builder whose advertisements he saw on the back cover of *Popular Mechanics*. When the magazine came in the mail, he would take it to his room and pore over the picture with warm, loving feelings. He doesn't know why, and a scientist won't be much help either. One thing seems clear: His experience was as natural and unplanned as mine was.

Some people don't remember having strong romantic fantasies; others have felt drawn to both sexes.

We don't know why, but one thing is clear: It's not a free or conscious choice.

As researcher Dr. Richard Green says of all this: "Falling in love is one of the great remaining mysteries."

* * *

QUESTION: Why Does So Much of This Research Involve Only Men?

Research grants and interest reflect the male orientation of science and of the society we live in. In 1990 and 1991, several surveys of medical research showed a clear statistical bias against research on women and women's concerns. Although little work has been done on male homosexuality, even less has been done on female homosexuality.

* * *

QUESTION: Is Homosexual Sex Unhealthy?

It can be—just as heterosexual sex can be. Sexual intercourse, including anal intercourse, can be the means of transmitting disease. (However, most of the world's people with the AIDS-causing HIV were infected through *heterosexual* sex. HIV in the United States spread first through the male homosexual community, but the rate slowed with changes in practice; most new cases are now spread by drug needles or heterosexual sex.)

Gay or straight, having more than one sex partner increases health risks. So do physical abuse, exploitation, possessiveness, and jealousy.

Not all gay men engage in anal sex, and among those who do, it is a small part of all that comprises sexual activity. But it seems to obsess some non-gay people, dominating their discussion of homosexuality out of proportion to the extent that it is actually practiced. Anal intercourse can be unhealthy without proper precautions. The anus or rectum can be torn; scrapes in the mucous membranes of the rectum can allow disease organisms—including HIV—to enter the blood stream.

Some diseases can also be transmitted by oral-genital sex, although the risk of getting AIDS this way seems to be a great deal less than in anal intercourse.

45

However, these facts are a precarious foundation on which to build a case against "the practice of homosexuality."

Kinsey found, and most people know by now, that anal sex and oral-genital sex are practiced by a high proportion of heterosexual people as well. Health precautions are well advised for all who practice them outside a committed, long-term, monogamous relationship.

*   *   *

QUESTION: What Does It Mean to Be a "Practicing" Homosexual?

Even the people who put the phrase *practicing homosexual* in the United Methodist *Discipline* are vague about this. Most were undoubtedly referring to sexual acts.

But it's important to think more deeply about the question, for two reasons:

1. There is a great deal more to a person's sexuality than what he or she does in bed. If we want to understand either homosexual or heterosexual people, we need to remember this.

2. Some people fall into the trap of deciding to "love the sinner but hate the sin"—accepting a person's homosexual orientation but demanding that he or she not *act* upon it.

To start working on the question, it might help to ask, "What does it mean to be a 'practicing *hetero*sexual?'" Just what is a heterosexual act? A glance? A wink? Holding hands? Watching someone of the other sex walk by, and being attracted? Touching someone on the arm? Embracing? In the 1950s, you weren't "having sex" until the moment of copulation; none of the rest, right up through "heavy petting," was sex—and thus was permissible.

It could be argued that putting on an earring is an act of sexuality—homosexual or heterosexual or neither, depending on whom you're dressing up for.

Is it the practice of homosexuality when one man pats another affectionately on the rump? Not if one is the quarterback and the other a lineman who just gave him a great block!

We are sexual beings. From the clothes we wear to the titles we bear, we are practicing our sexuality. Gay men, lesbians, and bisexuals raise a serious question for us when they ask, "How can you ask me never to express my feelings of love for another?"

If sexuality is God's gift, and if we accept the scientific consensus that our orientation is fixed very early, then it's difficult just to brush off their question.

Celibacy is fine as an option for any Christian. But Protestants don't see it as the highest choice, and when it is imposed by others, it is a perversion of God's good gift. It is asking gay men and lesbians to bear a burden that many of us are not willing to shoulder ourselves.

* * *

QUESTION: Aren't Some Children Seduced into Homosexuality?

No. Our sexual orientation is not "caught." Kinsey Institute researchers, affirmed by social workers and others, find no support for this.

It is sad that there are adults who will sexually exploit children. The vast majority (more than 90 percent) are heterosexual males abusing female children. Whatever the orientation, such abuse is wrong, and can cause long-lasting emotional harm.

But there is no evidence that it changes the victim's sexual orientation, one way or the other.

* * *

QUESTION: Can Gay People Be Cured or Change Their Ways?

There is strong evidence that sexual orientation is rarely if ever changed. Heterosexual or homosexual, we have little if any choice about the gender of the people we fall in love with. There are no studies in peer-reviewed scientific journals that claim to have changed a gay person's basic feelings.

Methods tried include shock therapy, aversion therapy, psychiatry, and hormones. Society has used persuasion, scorn, repression, and even marriage to get homosexual people to deny or repress their true feelings.

Some gay men or lesbians, torn between heterosexist pressure and their feelings, have sought help to change. There have always been people willing to help them change. But even the most eager of the ex-gay movements doesn't claim a change in orientation—just in practice.

And there does appear to be a choice in what we *do* with our feelings. Since the early 1970s, most psychotherapists have sought to help gay or lesbian patients accept themselves and function better in daily life. But among patients who came seeking to *change,* a few psychotherapists report some success in changing their overt behavior.

Scattered as we are along the Kinsey scale, there are many people who can be attracted to either sex. It's reasonable to assume that they can choose to practice either same-sex or other-sex behavior. Some may switch frequently, while others may choose only one type of practice for life.

The question that most of us have asked ourselves is "Why should we change?" We know that it is more natural for us to explore loving, responsible attachments to people of our own gender, and we know that the quality of these relationships is no better and no worse than those of the heterosexuals around us.

For most of us, the disadvantages of social non-conformity are far outweighed by the advantages of accepting and taking pride in who we are as whole human beings.

—*From "Twenty Questions about Homosexuality,"*
by the National Gay and Lesbian Task Force

*   *   *

QUESTION: Why All This Interest in Cause and Cure?

Can it be that there still are many people who have a subconscious commitment to the idea that the life of homosexuals cannot be anything but sinful?

The history of our attitudes toward gay men and lesbians shows what convenient scapegoats they make. When the church began reflecting these attitudes, it stated them in terms of sin. Homosexual people had *chosen* to be the way they are. If you believe in free will, as we Christians do, you feel that people are

49

responsible for the free and conscious choices they make. And you hesitate to identify as a sin something people have no choice about.

Thus, if we're to hang on to the idea that all homosexual activity is sinful, we'd better hope science can prove it's a matter of free choice and that homosexual orientation is not God-given.

There are lesbians and gay men hoping for the opposite—that science will find a single cause, confirming their lack of choice. But others fear that such a discovery would be used against the gay community, either in attempting a biological "cure" or in preventing the birth of people with a homosexual orientation.

A medical doctor, writing to "Dear Abby" about the recent research on twins, concluded with this:

> But, Abby, within our society, the origin of so much prejudice and hatred directed at gay men and lesbians is a far more critical issue than is the origin of sexual orientation. Prejudice is a tragedy for everyone. Parents of gay children needlessly agonize, and families are disrupted. Gay people suffer emotional and physical trauma. The talents of so many people are consumed in either perpetuating or fighting injustice. What we need is a war on prejudice—and if it is ever won, concerns about nature or nurture will become about as pressing as concerns about the origin of left-handedness.
>
> —*James Krajeski, M.D.,*
> *Corte Madera, Calif.*

* * *

QUESTION: Is Homosexuality Natural?

Natural has many meanings. If you're asking, have all cultures in all ages had people who engage in same-sex acts, the answer is, "As far as we can tell, yes."

If you're asking, is there same-sex behavior among animals, the answer is still yes.

Homosexual activity occurs under some circumstances in probably all known human cultures and all mammalian species for which it has been studied. The conditions under which it occur, and the probable or inferred meanings of the activity vary so widely that little authoritative consensus exists about when, or even whether, it ever represents clinical psychopathology.

—Warren J. Gadpaille, M.D.,
"Normal Human Sexuality and Sexual Disorders,"
in H. I. Kaplan and A. J. Sadock, eds.,
Comprehensive Textbook of Psychiatry

[After reporting same-sex arousal and activity in nineteen species ranging from antelope to lizards,] whether such biologic inheritance is an adequate basis for considering any activity right or wrong, socially desirable or undesirable, is an issue which we do not raise, and one which we have never raised. We do contend, however, that sexual acts which are demonstrably part of the phylogenetic heritage of any species cannot be classified as acts contrary to nature, biologically unnatural, abormal, or perverse.

—The Kinsey report, 1949, p. 24

* * *

QUESTION: Is Homosexuality a Mental Illness?

A large body of evidence indicates that it is not. A study for the National Institutes of Health gave psychological tests to adult homosexuals and heterosexuals, and was unable to differentiate between the two

51

groups on the basis of mental stability, creativity, or the ability to function in society.

There is evidence that the suicide rate is higher among gay and lesbian *youth* than among other teenagers. This is widely attributed to the pressures on people who are struggling with deep-seated feelings that society tells them are abnormal—right at the time when all young people are seeking a sense of identity.

But with adults, it appears to be different. The Pentagon ordered a study of homosexual people—including their mental health—in hopes it would provide a rationale for the military policy of booting gays and lesbians out of the services.

The study, released in 1988 by the Defense Personnel Security Research and Education Center, proved just the opposite, and an embarrassed Pentagon tried to suppress it. Its conclusion on mental health was

> that the range of variation in personal adjustment is no different from that of heterosexuals. A review of 14 major studies beginning with Hooker's (NIH) in-depth investigation (1957, 1965), gave no support to the hypothesis that same-gender orientation was a sickness.

Until 1973, most psychiatrists treated homosexuality as an emotional problem, based on the little research that was available. But that research had been done on the troubled people who came to psychiatrists for help; when new work was done with gay men and lesbians who weren't psychiatric patients, the data were quite different. Based on this change, the American Psychiatric Association and, later, the American Psychological Association, stopped regarding homosexuality as a disease.

* * *

QUESTION: I Hear About the Homosexual "Lifestyle." What Is It?

We might as well ask what the "heterosexual lifestyle" is. There isn't one pattern of living; there are as many as there are individuals.

The word *lifestyle* not only implies a single identical pattern for every gay person, but also *free choice* and *irresponsibility*. It thus isn't adequate to describe some 25 million people in the United States whose orientation has been given them, and who are as responsible or irresponsible as the rest of us.

Lifestyle stirs up visions of mean-looking, tough women and limp-wristed men, all compulsively sex-hungry and promiscuous.

* * *

QUESTION: Isn't the Practice of Homosexuality a Threat to Traditional Family Values?

How, exactly? This may be another of those phrases that sounds instantly sensible from a rabble-rousing member of Congress or a talk-show host but doesn't hold up past the first flush of emotion.

What do these rabble rousers have in mind? That if given a chance, so many people would flock to become gay or lesbian that heterosexual families would disappear for lack of interest? Hardly.

There is a breakdown in the stability, the integrity of the family. The "standard" family—with two parents, married for life—is now the exception, not the rule. That's a real loss; it is both a *result* and a *cause* of disruption in society at large.

But the practice of homosexuality is not what is

causing these unsettling changes. There are, in fact, three kinds of disruption of family values associated with gay people—and the cause in each case is homophobia.

The first was mentioned in the first chapter of this book: The family that is split when it rejects and isolates a gay child. The cause may be automatic responses learned by growing up in a bigoted world; it may be fear of what the neighbors will say; it may be fear of our own unexamined sexual feelings. One thing is sure: The cause isn't homosexuality, but an unreasoned reaction to it.

A second pattern of disruption comes when gay men and lesbians are driven into marriage by societal pressure. Don't think the pressure isn't there. Well-meaning parents or friends ask, "Why aren't you dating a nice boy (or girl)?" "(*Sigh*) I guess I'll never have grandchildren."

Rock Hudson and Charles Laughton aren't the only closeted people who married to protect their reputations. Hundreds of thousands have done so to please their families, or to convince themselves that the fantasies and urges with which they've been struggling can be overcome or "cured."

These weddings take place because society is telling one of the parties he or she isn't normal, isn't worthy.

Some of these marriages work even if the gay partner eventually comes to terms with his or her sexuality; often it becomes an affectionate partnership without sex. Sometimes the partner sublimates those feelings, at great cost, or lets them emerge only late in life.

More often than not, though, it's a doomed marriage, with divorce and intense suffering the result. The heterosexual partner feels victimized and rejected; the gay or lesbian partner feels guilt and the rejection of the unsympathetic world that drove him into this in the first place.

And the culprit isn't homosexuality; it's the overwhelming heterosexism with which we're surrounded.

The third breach of traditional values comes when two people who love and care for each other look for a way to declare their commitment before God and the community. Two such people have the full backing and enthusiasm of the church, with prayerful ceremony, joy, and good fun. They represent the basic family value: enduring, committed, monogamous love.

Unless they happen to be of the same sex. Then all bets are off.

Family values are breached all right, not by the couple, but by those who would keep them apart.

*   *   *

QUESTION: I Don't Know Any Gay People. How Do I Identify Them?

You don't identify them. If they trust you, they may come out to you. But you won't know them from the stereotypes—masculine women or effeminate men, for example. The Pentagon was interested in identifying gay men, as you might imagine; the study mentioned above concluded that "feminized males make up only a small proportion of homosexuals, perhaps 10 percent. Thus 90 percent . . . display no overt behavioral stigmata."

But unless you live alone on a desert isle, you probably do know gay people. They are your brothers and sisters, your children, your co-workers. They sit next to you in church and may be in the pulpit. Their interests and concerns are likely to be much like yours—job, finances, home life, love, some happiness.

At least one in every four families has a gay member. They are not "them." They are us.

Some of them you know because they're in history books, though you may not have known they were gay. They include the Dodger outfielder who invented the "high five," and the man who wrote the music for "Onward Christian Soldiers."

They include King Richard the Lion Hearted and Christina, a seventeenth-century queen of Sweden. Here are a few of them—lesbian, gay, or bisexual—who made themselves known, or lived in times when there was less stigma, or "came out" after death:

◆

Sir Benjamin Britten, composer/conductor
Sir Arthur Sullivan, composer of "Onward Christian Soldiers"
Leonard Bernstein, conductor and composer
Bessie Smith, blues singer
Janis Joplin, singer
Noel Coward, composer and entertainer
Peter Illyich Tchaikowsky, composer (*Swan Lake*, *1812* Overture)

◆

Pope Julius III

◆

Leonardo da Vinci, scientist, painter of *The Last Supper*

Michelangelo, sculptor, painter of the Sistine Chapel
Sandro Botticelli, painter

◆

Sir John Gielgud, actor
Charles Laughton, actor
George Sanders, actor
Rock Hudson, actor

◆

Willa Cather, novelist
Walt Whitman, poet
Emily Dickinson, poet
Tennessee Williams, playwright
Virginia Woolf, author
George Gordon, Lord Byron, poet
Hans Christian Andersen, author
E. M. Forster, author
W. H. Auden, poet
Malcolm Boyd, theologian and writer
Francis Bacon, philosopher and statesman
John Milton, author and poet
T. E. Lawrence, soldier and author

◆

Dave Kopay, San Francisco '49ers running back
Glenn Burke, Dodgers outfielder (1977 World
Series)
Bill Tilden, champion tennis player

◆

King Richard the Lion Hearted, English king

57

King Richard II, English king
King James I, who commissioned the King James translation
Queen Christina of Sweden
Gustavus III, Swedish king
Frederick the Great, Prussian king
Peter the Great, Russian czar

♦

Dag Hammarskjöld, Swedish UN secretary-general
John Muir, naturalist, father of the national park system
Alexander von Humboldt, popular German scientist, after whom the Humboldt Current is named, as well as at least one United States university and several of the United States' counties
Alan Turing, whose "Enigma" machine, precursor of the computer, broke the German military code in World War II
John Maynard Keynes, British economist
Malcolm Forbes, publisher

One of Stephen's favorite theories was that lesbians and gay men were survivors of an alien spaceship, and that someday our kind would find us and get us the hell out of here.

—*Obituary in the* Bay Area Reporter, *December 1990*

Chapter Four

What Does the Bible Say?

Did you know that women have one more rib than men do?

Funny. There was a time when everybody knew that.

Up through the fifteenth century, it said so in the crude medical texts. Healers knew it. Theologians and the man and woman in the street all agreed: Men had one less rib than women.

If anybody disagreed with this universally recognized "fact," they kept quiet about it.

It was unquestioned common knowledge—not because the scientists of the day had examined real cadavers and counted the ribs. It wasn't something discovered in the process of tickling a sweetheart—a practice almost certainly discovered by then.

And it wasn't because people in the Middle Ages were physically different from us, their descendants.

No, it was because the biblical scholars and church officials of the day felt the evidence in Genesis was clear: Eve had been made from a rib removed from Adam. Therefore Adam, and his male descendants, had to be short one rib.

Never mind that the interpretation ran contrary to easily verifiable fact. When science and the Bible appeared to conflict, the Bible won.

It wasn't until the sixteenth century that somebody dared question all this. The rebel was Andreas Vesalius, the first modern anatomist, and after careful study of bodies, living and dead, he was pretty blunt:

"The ribs are twelve in number on each side in man and woman," he wrote in his text on the human body, published in 1543. "The popular belief that man is lacking a rib on one side and that woman has one more rib than man is clearly ridiculous."

You can imagine the outraged response of church leaders. Vesalius was accused of being a revisionist, twisting the Scriptures to serve his own ends. Called a heretic, he narrowly escaped with his life for stating a fact anybody could have verified.

And it still was many years before the holy fathers changed official church policy on the subject.

* * *

This is the kind of mistake we seem doomed to repeat—and repeat—down through church history.

—We forget that the Bible's power is in its religious ideas, not in its science. Genesis was about God's creative love, not about anatomy.
—We forget that the Bible's power is in its great themes, relevant to every age—not in specific commands designed for a time and situation centuries ago. The priestly rules in Leviticus, which forbade the crossbreeding of cattle or the blending of cotton and wool in a robe, were set down at a time when the Israelites' identity as a

separate people was threatened—during or just
after the exile. Drawing clear boundaries was
crucial, symbolizing the line between the chosen people and the rest of the world.
—We repeatedly fall into the trap of *using* the
Bible—picking and choosing from its richness
those passages that appear to confirm the biases
of the institutional church or of the society around
us. In the fourth century, for example, when theologians were increasingly influenced by the
pagan idea that sex was evil, it was necessary to
believe that the Virgin Mary remained a virgin all
the rest of her life. Helvidius was condemned for
suggesting that Mary went on to have other children, even though his critics had to do some fancy
selecting—leaving out any mention of Jesus'
brothers, for example.

In America, the Scriptures were quoted to justify the
enslavement and slaughter of native Americans by
invading Europeans. Later, the owners of the 4 million
slaves of African descent found their justification in
the Bible.

Later yet, the Astors, Carnegies, and Morgans found
scriptural backing for immense fortunes based on
exploitation of others.

When I lived and worked as a civil rights worker
in the Mississippi Delta, 1965 to 1967, I had some
heartbreaking experiences. I met people in the cotton fields who had never in their lives had what we
would call an adequate meal. A baby died of malnu-
trition a few minutes after her mother brought her
into our office. Five acquaintances of mine were
killed for working nonviolently for their Constitu-
tional rights.

But it was almost as heartbreaking, as a clergyman brought up in the church, for me to learn that the accepted rationale for the whole system that produced these crimes was the Bible I had been taught to love and revere.

It wasn't just at the Klan rallies (although they opened and closed with prayer and scripture). The staid and powerful white churches, full of "moderates" who decried violence but dragged their feet on justice, also looked to the Bible for justification.

The real roots of slavery, and then of United States apartheid, were economic. But its defenders needed a more publicly acceptable—and more simplistic—reason. Somewhere during that 400 years of United States history, the Bible came to be interpreted as affirming and justifying what was being done to African Americans. The white church went along.

If you had been on the state capitol grounds in Jackson, Mississippi, on a certain Sunday morning in 1965, you'd have seen a strange sight. Across the street was a large church, and at the top of the front steps stood a row of white ushers, arms linked, barring the way to the doors.

There were four or five black men, conservatively dressed for church, standing on the lower steps, facing the doors. As one of these men approached the top step, an usher disengaged his arm and smashed the would-be visitor in the face, sending him sprawling down the steps.

Inside, the congregation was singing the opening hymn: "Love divine, all loves excelling. . . . "

How could they live with themselves? Well, the Bible says Noah's son Ham sinned, and his descendants must ever after pay the price. And Ham's descendants, somebody decided, were the world's people of color.

Twenty-five years later, you'd have a hard time finding anybody in Jackson willing to twist the Bible that way to justify racism. With embarrassment, we realize that we of the church were conforming to the world, rather than letting the gospel transform us.

But it looks as though we're not through making such mistakes. There are those who'll declare with absolute certainty that the ancient writers' attitudes toward homoerotic acts are perfectly applicable today. Those who disagree are "revisionists" or worse.

Many of us are willing to apply a selective double standard of biblical interpretation against gay people in the same ways we once did against minorities.

Like the nine-year-old Mets fan who thought the first words of Genesis were "In the big inning . . . ," we read into the Bible what we expect to see there.

* * *

QUESTION: But the Bible References Used to Justify Racism Were Vague. Isn't the Bible Much More Clear When It Condemns Homosexuality?

No more "clear" than it is about the place of women. Here's a newspaper advertisement that appeared in a small-town Iowa newspaper in 1991. It gives the impression of a pretty consistent and clear approach to women by the biblical writers:

SHOULD WOMEN PASTOR CHURCHES?

1. The office is to be desired by men (I Timothy 3:1).

2. The pastor is to be the husband of one wife (I Timothy 3:2). This is difficult for a woman.

3. The pastor must be a man that rules his house (I Timothy 3:4).
4. The pastor's wife must meet certain requirements (I Timothy 3:11).
5. The woman is not to teach or usurp authority over the man (I Timothy 2:11).
6. The woman is to keep silent in the church, which means she has no teaching or preaching ministry to men (I Corinthians 14:34, 35).
7. The woman is to be in subjection to her husband (Genesis 3:16 and Ephesians 5:22).

Liberal churches that do not believe the Bible is God's Word without error, would endorse woman preachers. Bible believing churches would not sanction such.

Most people who saw this advertisement were appalled that these verses were still being used to define women's role (and equally dismayed at the spirit in which they were used: The advertisement appeared the same week as the town's first woman pastor arrived to take up her duties).

Yet it hasn't been too long since this advertisement's message would have been considered biblical truth and would have been the majority opinion.

* * *

QUESTION: Then What Does the Bible Say About Homosexuality?

About homosexuality as we know it, the Bible doesn't say anything. Neither the biblical scribes nor anybody else writing in those centuries had any idea of what we call homosexual orientation—a life-long attraction, fixed early, toward people of the same sex. In fact, we didn't have a word for it until late in the nineteenth century, when psychological concepts were first being understood. K. M. Benkert came up with the word in 1869.

But the Bible does have several references to sexual activity between people of the same sex. Interestingly enough, the assumption of the writers is that these are heterosexual men or women, acting in a way contrary to their "nature."

* * *

QUESTION: But Aren't These References Consistently Negative?

Yes. Every mention of homosexual sex indicates that it is wrong. There isn't a favorable word anywhere in the Bible about same-sex acts.

True, the references are few, and homosexual practice isn't the main theme of any of these passages. But we have to take them seriously—not only because they have reinforced our attitudes toward lesbians and gay men, but because this is the Bible, "the primary source and criterion for Christian doctrine," and we have a duty to try to find out what it is saying to us.

One way to get at the meaning of each passage is to ask these questions about it:

1. What was the writer thinking about when he wrote a particular passage? What was his world like? What were the circumstances that made him bring up this subject?

2. What exactly was he trying to say to the people of his day? Do we have as accurate a translation as possible?

3. In view of this background, what does the passage say to us? What is the *core truth,* stripped of the details that were relevant only for the writer's own day?

4. What in the passage is consistent—or inconsistent—with the great themes of the Bible?

5. What can the Holy Spirit contribute to our understanding of the passage, through reason, experience, and tradition?

The United Methodist Church's 1988 *Discipline* (paragraph 69.4, "Our Theological Task") says:

> We properly read Scripture within the believing community, informed by the tradition of that community. We interpret individual texts in light of their place in the Bible as a whole.
>
> We are aided by scholarly inquiry and personal insight, under the guidance of the Holy Spirit. As we work with each text, we take into account what we have been able to learn about the original context and intention of that text. In this understanding we draw upon the careful historical, literary, and textual studies of recent years, which have enriched our understanding of the Bible.
>
> Through this faithful reading of Scripture, we may come to know the truth of the biblical message in its bearing on our own lives and the life of the world.

* * *

QUESTION: What Are the Bible Passages, Then, About Homosexual Acts?

There are three major sets of references, each with a different apparent purpose and a different context. This is a hasty treatment; see the bibliography for more.

The Tale of Sodom and Gomorrah

> The two angels came to Sodom in the evening, and Lot was sitting in the gateway of Sodom. When Lot saw them, he rose to meet them, and bowed down with his

face to the ground. He said, "Please, my lords, turn aside to your servant's house and spend the night, and wash your feet; then you can rise early and go on your way." They said, "No; we will spend the night in the square." But he urged them strongly; so they turned aside to him and entered his house; and he made them a feast, and baked unleavened bread, and they ate. But before they lay down, the men of the city, the men of Sodom, both young and old, all the people to the last man, surrounded the house; and they called to Lot, "Where are the men who came to you tonight? Bring them out to us, so that we may know them." Lot went out of the door to the men, shut the door after him, and said, "I beg you, my brothers, do not act so wickedly. Look, I have two daughters who have not known a man; let me bring them out to you, and do to them as you please; only do nothing to these men, for they have come under the shelter of my roof." But they replied, "Stand back!" And they said, "This fellow came here as an alien, and he would play the judge! Now we will deal worse with you than with them." Then they pressed hard against the man Lot, and came near the door to break it down. But the men inside reached out their hands and brought Lot into the house with them, and shut the door. And they struck with blindness the men who were at the door of the house, both small and great, so that they were unable to find the door.

Then the men said to Lot, "Have you anyone else here? Sons-in-law, sons, daughters, or anyone you have in the city—bring them out of the place. For we are about to destroy this place, because the outcry against its people has become great before the LORD, and the LORD has sent us to destroy it." So Lot went out and said to his sons-in-law, who were to marry his daughters, "Up, get out of this place; for the LORD is about to destroy the city." But he seemed to his sons-in-law to be jesting.

When morning dawned, the angels urged Lot, saying, "Get up, take your wife and your two daughters who are here, or else you will be consumed in the punishment of the city." But he lingered; so the men seized him and his wife and his two daughters by the hand, the LORD being merciful to him, and they brought him out and left him outside the city. When they had brought them outside, they said, "Flee for your life; do not look back or stop anywhere in the Plain; flee to the hills, or else you will be consumed." And Lot said to them, "Oh, no, my lords; your servant has found favor with you, and you have shown me great kindness in saving my life; but I cannot flee to the hills for fear the disaster will overtake me and I die. Look, that city is near enough to flee to, and it is a little one. Let me escape there—is it not a little one?— and my life will be saved!" He said to him, "Very well, I grant you this favor too, and will not overthrow the city of which you have spoken. Hurry, escape there, for I can do nothing until you arrive there." Therefore the city was called Zoar. The sun had risen on the earth when Lot came to Zoar.

Then the LORD rained on Sodom and Gomorrah sulfur and fire from the LORD out of heaven; and he overthrew those cities, and all the Plain, and all the inhabitants of the cities, and what grew on the ground. But Lot's wife, behind him, looked back, and she became a pillar of salt.

Abraham went early in the morning to the place where he had stood before the LORD; and he looked down toward Sodom and Gomorrah and toward all the land of the Plain and saw the smoke of the land going up like the smoke of a furnace.

So it was that, when God destroyed the cities of the Plain, God remembered Abraham, and sent Lot out of the midst of the overthrow, when he overthrew the cities in which Lot had settled. (Genesis 19:1-29)

Sodom has become so identified in our language and folklore with homosexual acts—"sodomy" and "sodomites"—that it's very difficult to study this strange passage without preconceptions. Most of us grew up believing that homosexual practices were the cause of the destruction of Sodom and Gomorrah.

But most recent biblical scholarship questions this idea. It is more likely that the fatal sin of Sodom was violation of the sacred trust of hospitality the Hebrew people were supposed to show to strangers. There are many other passages in the Bible that mention Sodom, and the sins that all but the most recent two denounce are selfishness, arrogance, and inhospitality (see Isaiah 1, Jeremiah 23, and Jesus' words in Luke 10:10-12). Ezekiel (16:49) says, "This was the guilt of your sister Sodom: she and her daughters had pride, excess of food, and prosperous ease, but did not aid the poor and needy."

"The real irony is that homosexuals have been the victim of inhospitality for thousands of years in the Christian nations of the world. Condemned by the church and the state, they have been ridiculed, rejected, persecuted, and even executed. In the name of an erroneous interpretation of the crime of Sodom, the true crime of Sodom has been continuously perpetrated to our own day."

—*Dr. Edward Bowman,*
United Methodist pastor who for more than 20 years
conducted a Bible class on television
in the Washington, D.C., area.

The Priestly Codes in Leviticus

You shall not lie with a male as with a woman; it is an abomination. (Leviticus 18:22)

If a man lies with a male as with a woman, both of them have committed an abomination; they shall be put to death; their blood is upon them. (Leviticus 20:13)

These were the laws aimed at keeping the Hebrew people pure and separate from other peoples—especially from those who worshiped idols and practiced the prostitution, both male and female, of the fertility cults.

As we've pointed out before, boundaries were crucial—between Hebrew and Babylonian, meat and milk, between kinds of cattle, and between men and women. Acts that violated the assigned roles of each sex were "abominations"—part of the same mishmash list as sowing two kinds of crop in the same field. (Those shrimp-and-steak dinners that look so good in the television commercials are out, too; both shellfish and rare steak are forbidden.)

Taking the priestly codes literally in the twentieth century raises some real problems. We don't feel condemned for wearing a shirt of 65 percent cotton and 35 percent Dacron, because that prohibition spoke well but specifically to a situation no longer meaningful.

We still deplore adultery, or cursing one's parents. But we don't apply the Levites' prescribed punishment: death by stoning.

If we try to apply these rules literally, it seems to me we must apply them all, not picking and choosing. And taking them literally puts us in conflict with a teaching far more basic to our faith—that the old law was replaced with the new grace in the coming of Jesus Christ:

> "Owe no one anything, except to love one another; for the one who loves another has fulfilled the law. The commandments, 'You shall not commit adultery; You shall not murder; You shall not steal; You shall not covet'; and any other commandment, are summed up in this word, 'Love your neighbor as yourself'; Love does no wrong to a neighbor, therefore love is the fulfilling of the law." (Romans 13:8-10)

Which brings us to the third set of passages about homosexual acts.

The Letters of Paul

For the wrath of God is revealed from heaven against all ungodliness and wickedness of those who by their wickedness suppress the truth. For what can be known about God is plain to them, because God has shown it to them. Ever since the creation of the world his eternal power and divine nature, invisible though they are, have been understood and seen through the things he has made. So they are without excuse; for though they knew God, they did not honor him as God or give thanks to him, but they became futile in their thinking, and their senseless minds were darkened. Claiming to be wise, they became fools; and they exchanged the glory of the immortal God for images resembling a mortal human being or birds or four-footed animals or reptiles.

Therefore God gave them up in the lusts of their hearts to impurity, to the degrading of their bodies among themselves, because they exchanged the truth about God for a lie and worshiped and served the creature rather than the Creator, who is blessed forever! Amen.

For this reason God gave them up to degrading passions. Their women exchanged natural intercourse for unnatural, and in the same way also the men, giving up natural intercourse with the women, were consumed with passion for one another. Men committed shameless acts with men and received in their own persons the due penalty for their error.

And since they did not see fit to acknowledge God, God gave them up to a debased mind and to things that should not be done. They were filled with every kind of wickedness, evil, covetousness, malice. Full of envy, murder, strife, deceit, craftiness, they are gossips, slanderers, God-haters, insolent, haughty, boastful, inventors of evil, rebellious toward parents, foolish, faithless, heartless, ruthless. They know God's decree, that those who practice such things deserve to die—yet they not only do them but even applaud others who practice them. (Romans 1:18-32)

71

> Do you not know that wrongdoers will not inherit the kingdom of God? Do not be deceived! Fornicators, idolaters, adulterers, male prostitutes, sodomites, thieves, the greedy, drunkards, revilers, robbers—none of these will inherit the kingdom of God. (I Corinthians 6:9-10)

Paul's mentions of same-sex acts are examples, illustrations, of a point he is making. They aren't the *subject* of the passages involved. Still, we can't dismiss his strong disapproval.

In the Romans passage, Paul is writing about rebellion against God and its consequences. The obvious result of this rebellion is estrangement from God, but Paul points out another result—that good and natural things become perverted. Religion and sex are among these good things, he says.

Scholars don't agree on just what sort of relationship Paul was writing about. Depending on how you translate the Greek, it could be temple prostitution or it could be male same-sex practices in general.

Scholars do tend to agree, however, that Paul is writing about straights—people he saw as heterosexual, going against their natural instincts and engaging in same-sex acts. (It's interesting to speculate: If Paul had known what we know now about sexual *orientation*, might he have been equally disapproving of gay people who went against their natures and engaged in heterosexual acts?)

Like many people of his day, Paul saw these acts by heterosexuals as "degrading passions" and "unnatural intercourse," because they violated the rigidly prescribed power roles of the two sexes. Woman's role was subjugation; for a man to take the passive role, as in some sex acts—to act like a woman—was to degrade his manly nature. Equally "unnatural" was for a woman to assume the dominant male role in sex.

Also interesting is the list of activities and attitudes Paul describes as wickedness among the rebellious people.

He says they were filled "with every kind of wickedness, evil, covetousness, malice. Full of envy, murder, strife, deceit, craftiness, they are gossips, slanderers, God-haters, insolent, haughty, boastful, inventors of evil, rebellious toward parents, foolish, faithless, heartless, ruthless . . . " (Romans 1:26-31).

Doesn't this list raise some serious questions about the heavy emphasis the church has put, from time to time, on homosexuality? Conservative caucuses have gone to their denominations' governing bodies with condemnation of gay love as their number-one agenda item—not just once, but time and time again.

By what process do they choose? How does it happen that a caucus has never gone to the United Methodist General Conference with the votes to condemn gossip, and forbid the use of denominational funds to promote it?

When was the last time you heard of a pastor being denied an appointment because of boastfulness?

Back to Paul. In reading Romans 1:18-32, did you notice he was leading up to a "therefore"—one we ignore when we make this the most frequently used anti-gay passage in the Bible? This passage, the punch line, follows immediately:

> Therefore you have no excuse, whoever you are, when you judge others; for in passing judgment on another you condemn yourself, because you, the judge, are doing the very same things. You say, "We know that God's judgment on those who do such things is in accordance with truth." Do you imagine, whoever you are, that when you judge those who do such things and yet do them yourself you will escape the judgment of God? Or do you despise the riches of his kindness and

73

forbearance and patience? Do you not realize that God's kindness is meant to lead you to repentance? But by your hard and impenitent heart you are storing up wrath for yourself on the day of wrath, when God's righteous judgment will be revealed. (Romans 2:1-5).

In the second passage of Paul on this subject (I Corinthians 6:9-10), his remonstrance is against sexual acts that exploit or harm a partner, ignoring his or her worth as a child of God. Few would disagree with his condemnation of such behavior, whether by gay people or straights.

* * *

QUESTION: Is That All the Bible Has to Say About Homosexual Acts?

Basically, yes. But one of the stronger arguments against gay people is based on the fact that a key passage *omits* any mention of same-sex practice. This is the creation story, told twice in Genesis.

Some theologians believe these accounts (especially 1:26-28) tell exactly what God's will is for human sexual activity. Male and female were made for each other, as part of God's design. They are to be fruitful and multiply. A monogamous marriage is the only acceptable arena for sexual intimacy (2:24) and any other pattern is sinful.

Same-sex love is not mentioned here and is thus considered to be outside God's will.

That's a heavy load to put on this passage. To advance this argument, one has to believe Genesis was written to be a set of ethical guidelines or rules applicable to every generation. And you have to believe that the writers were aware of—and ruled out—love between people of the same sex, whose natural attraction has been with them from their earliest days and who have known no other.

Most current scholars feel the Genesis accounts are an explanation, not a prescription—an attempt to tell us why humans act as they do.

In writing about these passages, I've only touched the surface of a deeply complicated question. But I've tried to be true to the most recent scholarship, a growing body of belief that each of these passages is so tied to a specific cultural situation that its relevance in condemning same-sex love today is in serious doubt.

There are dedicated and capable Bible scholars who believe this handful of verses represents a major trend in biblical thought—a core theme of the Bible. It could be. We all are searchers together, and none of us can claim a monopoly on the truth. But the momentum, as we learn more about how to get at what the Bible says, is clearly and overwhelmingly in the direction I've indicated.

There is a fourth area of scripture we should think about:

The Teachings of Jesus

Here we have no references. None of the four Gospels reports that Jesus had anything to say about homosexual acts.

This doesn't necessarily mean he had no opinion on the subject. But it's certainly fair to suggest that neither he nor his biographers considered it a very important concern.

What *does* have a bearing on this subject is a major message of Jesus' ministry—maybe *the* major message: reaching out to the exiles and outcasts, to the oppressed and rejected.

He said, in his reading at his home synagogue, that he had come to "bring good news to the poor . . . to proclaim release to the captives and recovery of sight to the blind" (Luke 4:18). He had been a hunted exile as a child, and associated with social outcasts throughout his ministry.

When Jesus condemned human behavior, it was likely to be self-righteousness and arrogance. If he never mentioned homosexual acts, he certainly spoke often of the hardness of heart of religious insiders. He clearly wished religious institutions would leave the business of judging to God.

* * *

QUESTION: But What About Sin?
Are You Suggesting That
There Are No Standards
for Sexual Conduct?

Not at all. Those who question the relevance of the passages used against gay people for centuries nonetheless feel there is plenty of biblical help in making moral decisions about sex.

God's love and grace, reflected in the life and sacrifice of Jesus Christ, and spelled out as major themes of the Bible, tell us what we need to know about loving relationships. There is a growing belief in the church that the test of such a relationship is not the gender of the partners, but its nature.

If it exploits, abuses, imprisons, it is wrong, whether it involves a long-time monogamous marriage or not. If it is truly loving, affirming, supportive—reflecting the grace of God—it can be a holy union, whether the church and society see fit to recognize it or not.

That, I believe, is what the Bible says.

*   *   *

QUESTION: Isn't There Anything on This Subject That the Bible Speaks Clearly On?

The Bible is clear about hate: Hate is wrong.

It is wrong to draw a circle around a group of people and hate them because they're in that group, whether the excuse is race, sex, ethnic origin, or sexual orientation.

This hate is wrong whether it comes out in physical attacks or murder, or is confined to a snicker, a silence, a coolness, or the figurative but real closing of doors—including the doors of the church.

There is nothing in the Bible that gives us permission to hate people because we think they are sinners.

Quite the contrary.

Chapter Five

What Does the Church Say?

The bishops had been challenged. The glove had been thrown down.

Meeting behind closed doors in a Denver hotel on November 16, 1978, the fifty or so active and retired bishops of The United Methodist Church were considering a message from the board of the Good News Fellowship, a conservative, largely southern caucus of United Methodists.

Caucus members had been involved, six years earlier, at the 1972 General Conference, in amending the Social Principles to declare "the practice of homosexuality" to be "incompatible with Christian teaching." Then at the 1976 General Conference the caucus had led a fight to tie up use of any church funds that might seem to "favor homosexual practices."

Now the Good News board was worried that the bishops weren't zealous enough about enforcing all this. The caucus was asking for a pronouncement from the bishops, expressing solid support for "the church's stand."

Not that there was any doubt what the council would say. There hadn't been any real debate within the council over the issue, and none was expected now.

One by one, several bishops rose to speak in support of the anti-gay phrase.

As they talked, Bishop Melvin Wheatley of the Rocky Mountain Conference began scribbling notes on Antlers Hotel stationery for a statement of his own.

Wheatley was the host bishop; etiquette required hosts to be hospitable and accommodating, he recalls. "The host was supposed to answer questions, not raise them."

But when he got the floor, it was to raise some serious questions:

> A part of the inescapable loneliness of life is that I cannot and do not know your story very well and you cannot and do not know mine.
>
> I therefore reluctantly share a most intimate part of my story with you at this time, not primarily as an argument in debate to affect the way you vote, but rather as a sincere effort toward helping you understand the way I'm going to vote.
>
> Because my story is what it is, I cannot approach any statement on homosexuality as basically a position on an academic, though highly emotionalized, subject to be indentified as an "It."
>
> I approach any statement on homosexuality as basically an intentional stance toward intimately personal relations involving "Thous."
>
> Whenever I am asked to permit my name to be attached to any public pronouncement on real and particular persons, not a pronouncement on a subject without a face, I do not hear the meanings of that pronouncement transmitted through the editorialized columns of any of our publications.
>
> I hear the meanings of that pronouncement transmitted through the eyes and ears of my great medical doctor Bill, who twenty-three years ago literally saved my life, and who before that and after that was one of Lucile's and my most cherished friends.
>
> I hear the meanings of that pronouncement through the eyes and ears of that superb pipe organist and high-

ly respected accompanist for an international concer-
tizer whose name every one of you would recognize.
Roy is that skilled accompanist and cherished friend.

I hear the meanings of that pronouncement transmitted through the eyes and ears of that midwest United Methodist parsonage preacher's kid Rhea, who in
personal charm, intellectual perception, and spiritual
endowment reminds us of Georgia Harkness, and who
is one of Lucile's and my most cherished friends. I hear
the meanings of that pronouncement transmitted
through the eyes and ears of Lucile's and my beloved
son, John, who from the earliest months of his life to
these moments has convinced us that we were provi-
dentially guided in giving him the name associated
with the beloved disciple.

Why do I hear the meanings of any public pronouncement on homosexual persons through the eyes
and ears of these persons? For one reason, because all
four have in common same-sex rather than other-sex
orientation.

That same-sex orientation is perceived by all of them
not as something they have learned and practiced like
piano playing, but as something they are, something
they recognize and affirm, like thumbprints and skin
color.

For a second reason that is substantive for me, I hear
the pronouncement of support for the negative part of
the wording on homosexuality through their eyes and
ears; because all four of them (and many of the millions
they symbolize) would read from our statement one
clearly intended meaning:

That in the judgment of the Council of Bishops, they,
as homosexual persons, are automatically eliminated
from eligibility as authentic Christians.

But there is a third reason I see and hear through
their eyes and ears. In my judgment and in Lucile's—
not necessarily in their own—if the total life of each
one of the four is set against the criteria of the gifts and
graces and fruits of the Spirit delineated in our New
Testament, indeed against the criterion of a life moti-
vated and pervaded by Agape love, each one of them
appears to me and to Lucile to be as close to authentic

Christian living as we would dare perceive ourselves to be.

This part of my story, experientially received and recorded, radically affects the way I hear the proposal before us to reaffirm the negative wording on homosexuality in the 1976 *Discipline*.

Its words sound brave and strong and all but believable to some when addressed to a highly emotional but crassly exploited subject. Yet the same words strike me as naive, harsh, and categorically false when addressed to the Bills, the Roys, the Rheas, and the Johns of my daily experience.

Therefore, not only is it impossible for me to consent to add my name to any public pronouncement as here proposed, but also, it is imperative for me, out of my own sense of integrity, to insist that any such public pronouncement with which I could be identified carry the unmistakable message that the vote that launched it was not unanimous.

* * *

QUESTION: What Is The United Methodist Church's Historic Stand on Homophilia?

The denomination's historic stand is silence.

Neither the Evangelical United Brethren nor the Methodists had an official statement that mentioned homosexuality before the 1968 merger that created The United Methodist Church.

Both churches had gay people serving capably as pastors and as top leaders and administrators. Their orientation was known to a few and guessed at by others but usually wasn't an issue. The churches reflected the attitudes of the general public: It was one of those "I'd rather not know" things, and was discussed only when someone insisted on it.

The dark side of this was that so many people had to go through life hiding some of their most meaningful thoughts and feelings.

The bright side, if there was one, was that the church hadn't developed the witch-hunt mentality that developed in the merged church in the 1970s and 1980s, when conservatives put quiet, but persistent, pressure on general boards and agencies to get rid of people suspected of being gay. Some boards, under the threat that the accusers would go public, caved in.

The same thing happened in local churches. On one day in 1987 a friend of ours was a highly regarded assistant pastor, praised by his senior pastor and the congregation. One day later he was jobless—fired and evicted from his parsonage—having been found to be gay.

Contrast that with the service of two of my childhood role models in ministry. They were two women who had met in the early 1930s at seminary (the United Brethren church had been ordaining women since 1896). The two always served churches together, taking an occasional year off to travel the annual conference together as evangelists. They always shared a parsonage, too, until death finally parted them.

They are buried together, with a single headstone that gives their names and says, "33 years in the service of the Lord."

The point isn't whether they had a same-sex orientation or not, or "practiced" homosexuality or not, but that nobody ever bothered to ask. Nobody seemed to care. They were known by the results of their ministry, which included hundreds of young people won for Christ and thousands of parishioners given warm pastoral care.

In today's suspicious climate, such a career together would have been impossible.

* * *

QUESTION: How Did the Church Arrive at Its Present Position?

When you hear oratory about the denomination's "historic stand," they're talking about an official position that—at the time this is written—is barely old enough to vote: less than twenty years.

It began with a committee that had been working hard for four years to create a statement of social principles for The United Methodist Church, bringing together the best ideas from each of the former denominations. The statement had been brought to General Conference, the legislative body that meets every four years (same year as the Olympics, and in the future, the same year as the Summer Olympics) to do church business.

It dealt with such controversial issues as war, economic justice, and human sexuality. There had been attempts to get the committee to avoid the tough issues, but Bishop James Thomas, the chair, pushed for facing reality.

The resulting document was a far-seeing one for its day. The sexuality section began:

> We recognize that sexuality is God's good gift to all persons. We believe persons may be fully human only when that gift is acknowledged and affirmed by themselves, the Church, and society.

It called everybody "to the disciplined, responsible fulfillment of themselves . . . in the stewardship of this gift."

After urging "the medical, theological, and social science disciplines to combine in a determined effort to understand human sexuality more completely," the paper had this paragraph:

> Although all persons are sexual beings whether or not they are married, sexual relations are only clearly affirmed in the marriage bond. Sex may become expoitative within as well as outside marriage. We reject all sexual expressions which damage or destroy the humanity God has given us as birthright, and we affirm only that sexual expression which enhances that same humanity, in the midst of diverse opinion as to what constitutes that enhancement.

After deploring commercialization of sex and calling for better sex education and more help for sexually abused children, the document added a paragraph raising the issue the church hadn't wanted to talk about before:

> Homosexual persons no less than heterosexual persons are individuals of sacred worth. All persons need the ministry and guidance of the Church in their struggles for human fulfillment, as well as the spiritual and emotional care of a fellowship which enables reconciling relationships with God, with others, and with self. Further we insist that all persons are entitled to have their human and civil rights ensured.

It was a compassionate and intelligent approach to a subject few people understood. But it led to heated debate on the vast floor of the conference, where somewhere around a thousand people were participating.

During the debate, this amendment was passed and added to the statement:

> . . . although we do not condone the practice of homosexuality and consider this practice incompatible with Christian teaching.

85

Those seventeen words, almost an afterthought in the eyes of many who were there, would become the foundation of a wall built over the next twelve years— legal brick by legal brick—to protect the church from what Jerry Falwell calls "this terrible sin" and "the zenith of human indecency."

* * *

QUESTION: After Two Hundred Years of Methodism, Why Did This Happen at This Time?

For one thing, it happened because of what was going on in the world in which the church exists.

Almost exactly three years earlier, around midnight on June 27, 1969, the gay rights movement had exploded into headlines. It was the gay version of the Boston Tea Party.

It happened in a Greenwich Village bar, during a routine police raid. Such harassment was standard in New York City. Gay men didn't have the wide choice of meeting places—including the churches—open to heterosexuals who wanted to make new friends.

The bars were among the healthier options, but the price was being rousted by a police "raid" every now and then. The raids had more to do with collecting payoffs from the bar owners than with wiping out same-sex romance, but the police were free with their nightsticks and with their name-calling as they herded the crowd out onto the sidewalk. The whole thing was a humiliation, added to all the other heterosexist pressures of society, that the patrons didn't need.

But for years they took it. There had been associations of lesbians and of gay men since the Roaring

Twenties; the first known gay organization, The Society for Human Rights, had been founded in Illinois in 1924. But these organizations worked quietly and had little effect on anybody but their own members.

What happened at the Stonewall Inn in Greenwich Village that June night was that the patrons fought back.

They threw bottles and coins and bricks at the raiding cops. They rocked the police cars. Somebody threw a garbage can through a window. Thirteen people were arrested. It was far less violent than many racial confrontations of the 1960s—in Watts or Detroit, for example—but it was unprecedented for the gay community.

There were a couple more nights of defiance, with the crowds in Sheridan Square growing each night as the word spread. By the time the weekend—and the riots—were over, the word had spread across the country, long before a movie called *Network* had made the idea famous: "We're not going to take it any more."

Since then, the history of homophobia in the United States has been told in two parts, "Before Stonewall" and "After Stonewall."

Twenty years later, *San Francisco Examiner* reporter Raul Ramirez would write that the riots "galvanized gay political and social currents and redefined forever the limits of what U.S. gay men and lesbians were willing to countenance" (June 4, 1989).

The activism unleashed by Stonewall grew, and suddenly the country's gay community was no longer something straight people could ignore. More people came out of the closet; lesbian and gay civil rights organizations were formed. The 6:00 news discovered gay people and their frustration.

All this had at least two kinds of effects. It spurred some people to do more thinking about this suddenly visible minority; undoubtedly it was one reason the United Methodists' committee on the Social Principles decided to have a paragraph on the subject.

But most people were dismayed, even frightened and angry. Those most upset were fundamentalist Christians who saw homosexuality, in Falwell's words, as "Satan's diabolical attack upon the family" and "a symptom of a sin-sick society" that will "not only have a corrupting influence upon our next generation, but it will also bring down the wrath of God upon America."

The more activity there was from the gay rights movement, the more fearful some people became. By the time United Methodist conservatives arrived at General Conference to debate the proposed Social Principles, they had had three years to worry about the growing movement.

* * *

**QUESTION: Is the "Incompatibility" Phrase
the Only Official Action
on This Subject in the *Discipline*?**

No, the process had just started. In 1976, spurred on by conservative and liberal caucuses, United Methodists across the country sent General Conference more than 5,000 petitions for legislation on homosexuality.

The conservative caucus had been working for four years on a simple agenda: maintain the 1972 statement and build on it. The delegates went along, voting to retain the statement in the Social Principles, and passing three pieces of legislation that forbade use of general church money to "promote the acceptance of homosexuality."

The Social Principles are guidelines, not legislation. But the conservatives, building on the "incompatibility" statement, now had some solid anti-gay legislation in the *Discipline:* the funding prohibitions.

These turned out to be powerful tools. More than once, they were used to prevent studies of homosexuality. One UMC seminary reportedly refused to admit two gay students on the grounds that it would be a violation of the funding ban. *The United Methodist Reporter,* an independent newspaper, gave the funding ban as a reason for refusing a classified advertisement that would have told gay United Methodists how to reach a support group. (The Social Principles statement that "all persons need . . . the spiritual and emotional care of a fellowship which enables reconciling relationships with God, with others, and with self" apparently did not come up in the discussion.)

And the last two UMC clergywomen's conferences have ruled out discussion of issues affecting gay people—because it might violate the funding ban.

"I solemnly believe that there was never an hour in the Methodist Episcopal Church when it was in so great danger as it is today."

—The Rev. Dr. James M. Buckley,
May 6, 1888, during several days' debate
against the seating of four women—
elected delegates from the Kansas, Minnesota, Pittsburgh, and
Rock River conferences.
Dr. Buckley's side prevailed;
the women were not seated at General Conference.

* * *

QUESTION: When Was the Ban on Ordination of Gay People Passed?

In 1980 the issue was still heating up. One of the denomination's national agencies had fired a staff member because she came out as a lesbian. Moving the other way, clergy of the New York Conference had voted to affirm the appointment of an openly gay pastor—and had been backed up on appeal by the denomination's "supreme court," the Judicial Council. Many saw this as a "states rights" issue, because the decision whether a person was fit for the ordained ministry had traditionally been the prerogative of annual conferences, not of General Conference.

Conservatives came to the 1980 General Conference in Indianapolis loaded for bear, ready to push resolutions that would keep gay men and lesbians from being ordained or appointed, from holding any office in a church, and even from being members of a church.

But the momentum had slowed; these and other anti-gay issues were voted down. In fact, the majority of delegates moved in the opposite direction, approving a footnote on moral standards for ordained ministers that said, in part:

> The General Conference affirms the wisdom of our heritage expressed in the Disciplinary provisions relating to the character and commitment of ordained ministers. The United Methodist Church has moved away from prohibitions of specific acts, for such prohibitions can be endless. We affirm our trust in the covenant community and the process by which we ordain ministers.

The 1984 General Conference spent more time on the ordination question than all the previous ses-

90

sions put together. Better organized than in 1980, the anti-gay caucus quickly got a phrase inserted in the *Discipline* requiring candidates for the ministry to agree to observe "fidelity in marriage and celibacy in singleness." The intent was to bar gay people from ordination, but the Judicial Council ruled almost immediately that the new language didn't do the job. Only the "Annual Conferences have the authority to decide whether candidates for ordination meet the disciplinary requirements," the council said.

Still in session, the General Conference then finally finished the job started by the floor amendment twelve years earlier. It passed a a revised version of the paragraph in question, stating in part:

> Since the practice of homosexuality is incompatible with Christian teaching, self-avowed practicing homosexuals are not to be accepted as candidates, ordained as ministers, or appointed to serve in The United Methodist Church.

* * *

QUESTION: How Were Gay United Methodists Reacting to All This?

Many gave up on the church, or on this church, at least. Others, amazingly, kept on working to make the church what it says it is: for all, and open to all.

The picture in my mind is of a big tile-floored room without a stick of furniture in it. It was the failed restaurant of a seedy Indianapolis motel, the only one in the city that would reserve rooms for a group of gay people and their supportive friends.

Every evening during the 1980 General Conference, there were forty to fifty of us sitting on the floor around the edges of the room, leaning against the walls.

Each reported on his or her assignment—trying to reach members of a legislative committee to lobby before anti-gay measures went to the floor.

There were college kids and people in their sixties. There were clergy and ex-clergy, seminary students and lay men and women. All had paid their own way from across the country in hopes of persuading the delegates not to exile them from the church.

They were professors, bookkeepers, organists, dishwashers, clerks, and business executives. Some were delegates. Those clergy who were "out" had either left the ordained ministry or said they were about to be ejected. One young man, a few months from graduation, said he wouldn't be returning to seminary because it seemed inevitable that a ban on ordination would pass someday. They took turns, around the room, telling stories of pain and rejection, of hope for the church and fear that there was no hope. Several just prayed out loud. Someone was crying; I couldn't see who. There was prayer, and occasionally somebody would start a song—a hymn or a chorus from youth camp, or maybe one of the new songs, sitting there, swaying together and singing softly:

> We are gay and lesbian people,
> And we are singing, singing for our lives
> . . . .
> We are gentle, angry people, . . .

There was cynicism and despair there, along with the hope against hope. But I didn't sense any hatred, of the kind I'd seen on the faces of some delegates during the day's debate.

Virginia and I—the only self-avowed, practicing straights in the room—felt welcome, not rejection.

I couldn't help thinking that it was a model of what a church could be like.

*   *   *

Bishop Wheatley's colleagues listened politely to his statement in Denver in 1978, but the council maintained its support for the anti-gay language in the Social Principles.

Over the next few years, while he served as bishop of the Rocky Mountain Annual Conference, he and Lucile continued to speak out on behalf of gay and lesbian people, continuing their long history of advocacy of human rights causes.

These activities so enraged some conservatives that three United Methodist churches in Georgia and one in Texas filed charges against Bishop Wheatley.

They accused him of disseminating "doctrines contrary to the established standards of doctrines of the Church." They charged that he had "undermined the authority of Holy Scriptures, and repudiated the Scriptures, together with traditionally held interpretation of important Christian doctrines, including that of sin."

They said that Bishop Wheatley's statements were "divisive and thwart the evangelistic efforts of the Church."

The Western Jurisdiction Committee on Investigation had the duty of investigating the charges and deciding whether there should be a church trial.

The committee did not bring the bishop to trial, ruling that on this and another charge brought by a Boulder, Colorado, group that it was "fully satisfied that there is not reasonable ground for such accusations."

The committee added that it was not clear "whether the Social Principles provide a basis for chargeable offenses." It pointed out that, according to the preface

93

to the Principles, they are intended to be "instructional and persuasive in the best of the prophetic spirit. The Social Principles are a call to all members of The United Methodist Church to a prayerful studied dialogue of faith and practice."

Though the committee did not say so, the interpretation raises for many people the question as to whether the Principles are a strong enough foundation for the hard-line legislation passed since 1972.

The charges had been brought by churches as far as 2,000 miles away from Bishop Wheatley's Rocky Mountain Conference, and led to widespread discussion across the church. During that discussion, a colleague wrote, in a letter to *The United Methodist Reporter*:

"The church does include in its company many men and women, both laity and clergy, who are homosexuals. They deserve more than to be told to go away and leave us alone. They deserve more, in fact, than to be told that they are acceptable colleagues only if they will affirm the lifestyle of their 'straight' colleagues and abandon any semblance of their own sexual identity.

"As Bishop Wheatley has suggested, we need careful study of Scripture, for the evidence of homosexuality there is not as clear-cut as some assume it to be. We need far greater understanding of the psychological and physiological issues involved: i.e., that homosexual people are involved in something far more complex than a conscious choice of lifestyle that is totally a result of their own wills. And we need a great deal less recrimination and a great deal more effort to understand all who are party to this growing dialogue.

"I fear that for some in our church this has become a 'cheap' issue: one over which people who need not deal directly with homosexuals themselves, can get very emotional and about which they can feel very self-righteous, without any real cost to themselves. Some of those most indignant over the presence of homosexuals in the church seem relatively unconcerned about sexism, racism, the threat of nuclear war, questions of social and economic justice—a long list of concerns that, it seems to me, are of far greater consequence in our midst than a person's sexual identity."

—*Bishop R. Marvin Stuart,*
June 25, 1982

Chapter Six

What Is Our Ministry to Gay People?

A mother writes:

It was 1979; I was just out of seminary, after a career in nursing education. I was serving my first appointment, still a probationary member working toward ordination as an elder.

Just as I was leaving for a church weekend retreat, Bruce's and my twenty-two-year-old son, Phil, came by and said he needed to talk.

He said he'd be leading a discussion on human sexuality that Sunday at the church he attended, and had decided to share with the congregation a crucial and troubling part of his faith journey: the difficulty of being a closeted gay person in the church community.

He was "coming out" for the first time, and he was afraid his being gay might somehow hurt my chances of becoming ordained as an elder.

I had felt for a long time that Phil was gay but had waited for him to tell me. So it was a relief when he did. No more pretending, covering up, not being able to respond to his pain because neither of us could acknowledge that it was there.

I'd had several years to prepare for this moment, to read what I could find on homosexuality, and to be aware of how little help the church had been in understanding not only his, but my own sexuality.

Phil and I hugged and cried a little, and I assured him that his coming out wouldn't affect my ministry or the ordination process, and that it made no difference in my love and appreciation for him.

I hurried off to the retreat, and as I drove I realized I *was* anxious about the effect this news might have on my congregation. I needed to talk to somebody about it.

During a break in Saturday's schedule, I quietly shared the news with a clergy colleague I trusted, one who had seemed sensitive on other justice issues.

The man's first reaction was physical. *He began edging away from me.*

It was as though I had leprosy. (Keep in mind that this was two years before the first publicized case of what we now call AIDS.) There was no empathy, no feeling for my anxiety. He was edging away emotionally as well. "You'd better not let the congregation know that," he said. "That's just opening a whole can of worms, unnecessarily."

He made a couple of inane comments, told a joke about being gay, and changed the subject. I felt betrayed.

Those were the first of many valuable things I was to learn about the church and homosexuality: the lack of support for the families and the inability of many clergy even to talk about the human beings involved.

Later, as I ministered to other such families, I realized it goes further than lack of support. It includes burdening these families with guilt, while denying them an atmosphere where they can freely share their feelings about it with fellow Christians.

—The Reverend Virginia Young Hilton

The thing that impressed me most, however, and moved me deeply was the discovery of the incredible amount of suffering experienced by homosexuals. For centuries the church refused to serve them Holy Communion. They were often stripped, castrated, marched through the streets, and executed. In Hitler's Germany they were exterminated by the thousands in the furnaces and gas chambers.

In our own country, gay persons are disowned by their families, ridiculed and rejected by society, made the object of cruel jokes, and forced to laugh at the jokes lest their "secret" be revealed.

They are barred from jobs and housing, often living in loneliness, seeking companionship in sordid places and in devious (and dangerous) ways. They have become the "lepers" of our society. How many young people are there who lie awake at night, terrified by these "feelings," with no one to talk to?

—Dr. Edward W. Bauman,
UMC pastor and Bible teacher

99

* * *

QUESTION: Why Does the Church Have to Get Involved in This at All?

The Great Commandment and the Great Commission won't let us stay out of it.

We give lip service to the idea that God's love is unlimited, but find it hard to live out the great commandment—love God, and your neighbor as yourself. Jesus had a way of showing us who our neighbor is— the woman at the well, the tax collector, the woman taken in adultery, the leper—and made it clear that whether we were dealing with sinners or not, we were to *love* them. Not from afar, either: The Great Commission says, *Go*, ye, therefore.

* * *

QUESTION: But Isn't the Practice of Homosexuality a Sin?

Suppose it were. It still would make no difference in the love we are to have for people—all people.

Jesus made another thing clear—one of the most-quoted and most easily forgotten truths in Scripture: All of us are sinners, and our only salvation is in the loving grace of God, expressed through Jesus Christ. None of us is more "deserving" than anybody else.

D. T. Niles, great world evangelist, said evangelism is "one beggar telling another where to find bread."

That's the attitude with which the church's ministry to gay people must begin.

* * *

QUESTION: Why Is There Such Furor Over the Ordination of Gay People?

Some of it must be derived from two common untruths about homosexuality: that it can be "caught" and that homosexual people are out to seduce straights.

People are afraid a gay pastor will be a role model for their children, leading them into same-sex orientation. Or they know someone who was fondled as a child by an adult homosexual person. They don't want such unhealthiness in the pulpit.

But the verifiable truth is that sexual orientation is not something people choose. Experiences, positive or negative, have not been proven to change orientation. Gay couples who rear children have exactly the same percentage of gay children as the estimate in the general population.

In fact, turning these charges around is one way of showing how unreasonable our view can be:

WHY HETEROSEXUAL MEN SHOULD NOT BE ORDAINED

1. According to divorce statistics, fewer than half of them are able to maintain a long-term relationship.
2. The literature is full of tales of clergymen becoming sexually involved with women of the congregation.
3. Three out of four straight males in the United States admit being unfaithful to their long-term partners.
4. Thousands of straight men are in jail for molesting little girls. A shocking percentage of these victims were their own daughters.

5. Straight males are the driving force behind the declaration of wars—the only other activity described in the Social Principles as "incompatible with Christian teaching."

6. Jesus saved his harshest words for the self-righteouness of groups like the Pharisees and Sadducees—which, if they lived according to the code they promoted, were made up of straight males.

Is it reasonable to urge openness and love for a group of persons, while firmly rejecting them as clergy?

When the press discovered, a few years ago, that African Americans were allowed to be Mormons but not Mormon priests, there was an avalanche of criticism. Not long afterward, a new revelation was received, and African Americans were allowed into the priesthood.

That still left another whole class of "ineligibles" for the Mormon priesthood: women.

Pointing our finger at the Mormons, while we maintain a prohibition against ordaining gay Christians who feel called by God, makes us all "practicing" hypocrites.

In a body that celebrates the priesthood of all believers, we need to be aware of inconsistency when we say, "You are acceptable as a fellow pilgrim in my faith journey, possibly even as a friend, but not as a pastor."

* * *

QUESTION: Why Are We Being Asked to Perform "Holy Unions"?

The church has its gay members in a real Catch-22. One of the main sources of our criticism is the perception that promiscuity is an essential part of being gay. (It's not true of everybody; it may be true of only a small minority. Recent studies show a high percentage of gay men—as many as half—involved with just one partner. The figure is higher among lesbians.)

But at the same time we're putting down gay men for having multiple partners, we're also refusing to provide any support whatsoever for long-term monogamous partnerships.

My friend Jean Barnett and her longtime partner Ellie Charlton were attending a church meeting and were seated with two pastors from "transforming" congregations.

"Could Ellie and I join either of your churches without seeking to change our orientation?" Jean asked.

No, both pastors said. Then one added, brightly, "But I wouldn't take in a *straight* couple either, if they were unmarried like you."

Ellie shot right back: "Then will you marry us?"

Embarrassed, the pastor just shrugged.

Practice varies widely across the church, but pastors are performing "celebrations of commitment" or "holy unions" for same-sex couples. Sometimes it is with the knowledge and silent approval of a district superintendent or bishop.

The rationale is simple: God's love is best reflected in a committed, monogamous relationship. Making the commitment public and seeking God's blessing on it is one way that heterosexual partnerships are strengthened. Why withhold such help from a couple because they're the same sex?

* * *

QUESTION: Shouldn't We Concentrate on Helping Gay People Change?

Many people think so. The ex-gay movement—more than 60 organizations around the country—works with gays and lesbians who want to change their orientation or their practice. The ultimate proof of this change is seen as getting married and having children.

Bob Davies, executive director of Exodus, an umbrella organization for these ministries, says, "We are everywhere, in large and small churches and cities across the nation. We are a significant minority. The bottom line is we don't believe homosexuality is part of God's plan for our lives." Davies says the ministries have counseled more than 100,000 people.

* * *

QUESTION: Why Would Anyone Object to the Ex-Gay Movement?

There are many reasons for concern. First of all, many gay people quite rightfully resent being told by fellow Christians—all of whom have sinned and fallen short of the glory of God—"We'll accept you if you change, or at least try to change." The pastor of a transforming congregation told me he would not accept a gay man or lesbian as a church member unless he or she was seeking to become heterosexual. This is not only the self-righteousness of the Pharisees, it's not in the *Discipline*. General Conference has consistently resisted attempts to bar membership to homosexual people.

Second, many of these movements involve people who, despite their protestations of love, make no pretense of being free of homophobia.

The Reverend Louis Sheldon, a California minister, organized a "summit" in 1990 for practitioners of "reparative therapy"—converting gays to straights. He said the meeting's purpose was to "preserve heterosexuality as the norm for the U.S.A." and show the healing effects of reparative therapy. "We love the sinner and hate the sin" is a typical truism at such meetings.

But a few months later, when the California Legislature was considering legislation confirming that gays and lesbians were entitled to the same civil rights as the rest of us, Sheldon was among the most active of the bill's opponents, busily rounding up clutches of preachers whom he would produce in the hearing room to testify against it.

Whatever *loving the sinner and hating the sin* means, no responsible person believes it means withdrawing the guarantees of the Constitution from said "sinner."

Robert Bray of the National Gay and Lesbian Task Force expressed the concern:

> They present us as sick or deranged individuals that need to be changed to fit a heterosexual society. Exodus has set their sights wrong. What should be changed is their intolerance of gays and lesbians. What is interesting about Exodus is . . they don't overtly bash us. It's like a lovefest of bigotry and intolerance. It's homophobia with a happy face.

Third, "reparative therapy" not only defines the subject as less than acceptable, but cruelly sets up expectations that can't be met.

Bryant Welch, executive director for professional practice with the American Psychological Association, issued a statement in response to Sheldon's "summit" that said in part, "Efforts to 'repair' homosexuals are nothing more than social prejudice garbed in psychological accoutrements."

American Psychiatric Association spokesman Howard Marvantel said the "therapy"

can do more damage to a person's psyche than good. They do a lot of confrontational shouting, saying the person will go to hell. . . . It can cause future need for psychiatric help. It will cause a whole new level of guilt when you go back to your old life.

There is evidence that some homophilial people have changed their *practice* to heterosexual. But there are no five-year follow-up studies in the scientific literature to tell us what becomes of these people.

And there is no evidence that either straights or gays have been helped to change their *orientation*. A young man I know often testifies that a "transforming congregation" helped him "leave my homosexuality behind." He points out that he is now married and a father. But he also admits a continuing struggle with his strong erotic feelings toward men.

One of the "stars" of the ex-gay movement, who later left, was John Evans, a devout Christian who helped start the first of the ex-gay ministries, Love in Action.

"In my heart, I thought that being gay was a one-way ticket to hell," he told a reporter for the *San Francisco Examiner.* "I gave up everything to become an ex-gay, including my lover of fifteen years."

Evans was a counselor for Love in Action for three years, and was featured in one of its publications.

"People would come out here on the bus and train trying to get the cure. Parents would send their kids on a one-way trip here. If I was to try to be ex-gay all my life

I would have. But I came to realize that you could be gay and be Christian.

"Most of the people in these ex-gay groups are holding on with white knuckles, trying not to be tempted. It's all about trying to be something that they're not. Many try so hard to change. And when they don't make it, the ministry condemns them."

While Evans was a counselor, his friend Jack McIntyre also joined Love in Action. A product of conservative Christian teaching, the forty-five-year-old businessman believed homosexuality was sinful. He tried hard. But after a year, he saw that it wouldn't work. He killed himself, leaving a suicide note that said, "To continually go before God and ask forgiveness and make promises you know you can't keep is more than I can take. I feel it is making a mockery of God and all He stands for in my life."

Evans, 55, now an artist, says of McIntyre: "He wanted desperately to reconcile his spiritual side with his sexual side. I spent the last day of his life with him. He said he tried but he couldn't. He would be alive today if he realized that God loved him as he was."

Or if there had been church members willing to love him as he was.

* * *

QUESTION: What Is the Reconciling Congregation Program?

This is a growing movement across The United Methodist Church, with more than fifty churches and half a dozen annual conferences engaged in reconciling ministry with gay, lesbian, and bisexual people.

I believe it's a movement on sounder biblical ground than the ex-gay movement, which typically requires gay people to change before they are accepted.

The basis is Romans 5:10, "While we were enemies, we were reconciled to God." As the late Dr. Joseph C. Weber of Wesley Theological Seminary interpreted the passage in the first issue of the Reconciling Congregation journal:

> We were not reconciled to God because we deserved it nor were we reconciled because some of us were better or more moral than others. No, all of us were enemies of God. God, however, has reconciled us—God's enemies.

Each of the Reconciling Congregations has gone through a process of Bible study, prayer, and information sharing, taking as much as two years to decide whether to publicly state their openness to homophilial people in all activities of the church. The study process has meant growth for the people involved, many of whom started out suspicious of or antagonistic toward gay people.

The churches have grown too—an average of 30 percent in the year after becoming a Reconciling Congregation. Some of this growth, by no means all, has come from gay people hungry for a welcoming congregation. A truly open congregation apparently has appeal to all ages and persuasions, because they are included in the growth. The churches tend to be involved in many social concerns and social justice issues, not just opposition to homophobia.

It's an ideal model for ministry, involving the whole congregation as a community of love, examining the church's responsibility and the people's needs.

QUESTION: Our Church Isn't Ready to Think About Such a Step; Isn't There Room for Other Ministries?

Of course. Most churches are in your shoes.

One place to start is in the adult education ministry—maybe with a series on The Social Principles, or on "Issues Where Christians Differ." In a church where fear of the issue runs deep, it can be less threatening to discuss homophobia and homosexuality as one of a whole range of social justice issues, rather than all by themselves.

One church took on the topic, "The Social Principles: What Do They Mean for the Ministry of Our Congregation?" In each subject area, members found specific unmet needs in their own town. When it came to homosexuality, the needs are spelled out pretty clearly: the ministry and guidance of the church in their struggles for human fulfillment; spiritual care; and emotional care of a fellowship that enables reconciling relationships with God, with others, and with self. For that church, the start was a small, informal "gay/straight dialogue," one evening a month, where people could express their concerns and ask questions of one another. Some were really searching; some at first were hostile, on both sides. But the chance to talk opened minds.

If your church doesn't have any "out" lesbians or gay men, find one or two who are willing to meet with your class or group. The pastor of a Metropolitan Community Church often is willing and experienced in fielding questions. "Importing" guests is artificial, but sometimes gives church members their first face-to-face meeting, of which they are aware, with a lesbian or gay man.

109

Doing this, at some time in your study, is crucial; trying to study the issues with no gay person just reinforces the impersonality, the anonymity that lets us treat the whole thing as an abstract, rather than as an issue of justice involving our children, friends, and neighbors. (If you're sure your church isn't ready for this, then try to find a parent of a gay person who'll meet with your group. Parents and Friends of Lesbians and Gays (see address under resources) can put you in touch with such couples, who are often eager to help.)

Pastoral ministry, in the sense that it involves all of us believers, needs to reach out to three groups: gay people, many of them children of church families, who have left see the church because they see it as an oppressor, not a source of strength and comfort; families, especially parents, of lesbians and gay men; the members of your congregation who are most vocal against gay people.

Each of these groups has some obvious needs; the difficulty is not in ministering, but in *finding the will to be in ministry.*

But in each of the three groups there is an ache. Many gay people upon whom the church has turned its back find fulfillment in other denominations, other faiths, other non-religious activities. But the response to the reconciling congregations shows there are still many longing for "a fellowship which enables reconciling relationships."

With families, it takes only a signal from the pulpit or in the church newsletter to let people know they are not judged by the church—by *your* church, anyway. A pastor who mentions a gay acquaintance in a non-pejorative way, or includes gay men and lesbians in the list on Human Rights Day, will find parents quietly expressing thanks, and maybe asking to talk.

The anti-gay people may be harder to reach. Their self-righteousness is reinforced by society and by cults and caucuses that make a great deal of their money from homophobia —trumpeting the "threat" from homosexuality and offering, for a donation, to hold it at bay. But these too are people of sacred worth, and if there's a will, many can be reached.

AIDS ministries. AIDS is not a "gay" or "straight" disease; it is a virus spread by blood, semen, or vaginal secretions to anyone exposed to them. Most of the world's people with the AIDS-causing HIV are women and children. But in the United States, the disease was introduced through the gay community, and most of our people with AIDS are gay men.

The church has a long history of compassion for the sick, and there are congregations who have found that a ministry to people with AIDS has an unexpected side-effect: easing their fears of gay people. The need is great, and will increase as people infected as long as 10 years ago succumb to chronic illness or death. Needless to say, it must be a ministry without any of the judgmental baggage gay people have learned to expect from many church people.

> Judgmentalism never helps a person find forgiveness and healing; it only sends a message of disgust and rejection. People with AIDS especially feel the judgment of society. They quickly divide their world into those who accept them and those who reject them.
> —*Michael J. Christensen*
> The Samaritan's Imperative

Two reminders about ministry: First, the needs of gay men, lesbians and bisexual people, as spelled out in The Social Principles, basically aren't any different than anybody else's. It's we who have made a special case of them, usually in a destructively negative way.

111

Second, don't expect a big rush of grateful candidates for membership. After centuries of turning our backs, it'll take some work to prove that our motives are good and our pledges trustworthy. But it can be done. Arthur McBride, who reported the pain of being rejected by the church he grew up in (see p. 20), is now an active member of Edgehill United Methodist Church in Nashville—one of the Reconciling Congregations that set out to make every child of God welcome—and seem to be succeeding.

Chapter Seven

Can Homophobia Be Cured?

A father writes:

Typically, the parent of a gay child passes through successive stages of shock, disbelief, sorrow and, sooner or later, acceptance.

For many of us, however, there is yet another phase: outrage against society's stereotypical thinking that would relegate our gay loved ones to second-class citizenship. . . .

My daughter is a lesbian. She also is the light of my life, a warm and talented young woman whose joyous spirit helps brighten the lives of others. Ironically, she is now an even better person for having learned to live honestly and openly in a hostile society. . . .

. . . As I pondered the strength of the parent-child bond and the sheer numbers of homosexual Americans, I could envision the doom of homophobia's reign.

It is estimated that there are upward of twenty-five million gay people, who by defi- nition started out with some fifty million parents. Sooner or later, a large portion of those parents will want to enlist in the crusade for their children's dignity. When that happens a significant slice of the nation's voters, fired by familial bonds, will be dedicated to the most basic of free- doms: the right to be what one is.

—Robert A. Bernstein,
retired Justice Department lawyer,
in the New York Times

We have seen that homophobia is illogical and hurt- ful, not just to lesbians and gay men, but to all of us. As individuals, we have it deep in our subconscious, and it is woven into the structure of our society and the church.

It may not be curable.

It's the same struggle we have with racism and sex- ism: No matter how alert and sensitive we try to be, there's always another layer of discrimination to peel away.

* * *

QUESTION: When Feelings Are So Deep, and So Universal, Is There Any Hope of Change?

Yes, there is.

Some day, if you're lucky, you might be driving down through California's Owens Valley. On your right as you drive south will be one of the highest mountain escarpments in the world—a direct rise from the valley floor at 3,000 feet above sea level to the summit of Mount Whitney, at 14,700 feet.

Watch for a small sign on the right, a few miles south of Bishop. It will say Manzanar.

There's not much there now. A stone guardhouse. Concrete slabs that once held rough military-type barracks. Some rock gardens, their patterns still visible after fifty years of ceaseless wind and gritty dust.

Near the guard house, stop to read the bronze plaque bolted to a cemented pile of rock. This is part of what it says:

MANZANAR

In the early part of World War II, 110,000 persons of Japanese ancestry were interned in relocation centers by executive order No. 9066, issued on February 19, 1942.

Manzanar, the first of ten such concentration camps, was bounded by barbed wire and guard towers, confining 10,000 persons, the majority being American citizens.

May the injustices and humiliation suffered here as a result of hysteria, racism, and economic exploitation never emerge again.

And in the background, so near and yet so far, the pure-white glistening mountains, rising two miles straight up, speaking of beauty and freedom and God.

How did it happen? War hysteria, fear, racism—many things. But I can tell you that only a handful of people in the whole country raised their voices against it.

People like Governor Earl Warren and President Franklin D. Roosevelt, now heroes to liberals like me, not only went along but pushed hard to lock up these tens of thousands of innocent citizens.

Eventually we woke up. In the 1990s, we're trying to atone for the act with small reparations checks. The vast majority of Americans now think we made a serious mistake.

It took a 180-degree change by 99 percent of the population, but we did change.

We can learn from our mistakes; we can change, even if the change isn't as much as we'd like.

A 1991 study, reported in *The New Republic*, found that acceptance of gay people is higher than support for racial integration was forty years ago.

A Gallup Poll the same year found that 60 percent of the public believes gay men and lesbians should be allowed to serve in the military.

Little steps. Mixed signals. But hopeful signs.

*   *   *

QUESTION: How Do We Get Started on Change?

In looking for an answer, there are striking parallels in the struggle many people have with another devastating disease: alcoholism.

In homophobia, as in alcoholism, the most difficult step in a cure is recognizing and then admitting that we have the disease.

The matter of recognition is crucial. The most serious barrier to curing bigotry is realizing that we all are bigots.

As easy as it would be to point to other parts of the country, or other social groups, the fact is that each of us has taken the poison and suffered the weaknesses of discrimination.

One of the most revealing learning experiences for me in two years as a civil rights worker in Mississippi was that nobody I met—even at Klan rallies—ever believed he or she hated black people.

Those white Mississippians who worked hardest against change also protested hardest that they were not prejudiced. They sincerely believed it.

The second step is realizing, as in alcoholism, that while we probably never can consider ourselves cured, we can all be "recovering" homophobes. We can keep working on it.

The third essential is knowledge—especially personal, firsthand acquaintance with gay people. If you're lucky like me, you have somebody in the family to introduce you to gay people. If your church is lucky, gay people will visit; your welcome for them will more than be paid back. Knowing gay people has been the most valuable resource in fighting my own homophobia.

A *San Francisco Examiner* poll of married couples of child-bearing age found that the people least likely to reject a gay child were the ones who already knew a gay person.

> Knowledge—that is, education in its true sense—is our best protection against unreasoning prejudice and panic-making fear, whether engendered by special interest, illiberal minorities, or panic-stricken leaders.
>
> —*Franklin Delano Roosevelt*

The fourth essential is to keep dialogue going. Having strongly held opinions needn't keep us from talking with those who disagree. If we can't do that in the church, where can we?

> Though we cannot think alike, may we not love alike?
> May we not be of one heart though we are not of one
> opinion?
>
> *—John Wesley, in his sermon "Catholic Spirit"*

As individuals, what we're after is a paradigm shift—looking at the subject from an entirely different angle. An "aha!" An example of a paradigm shift is the story is told of a driver, winding his way up a narrow mountain road, suddenly confronted with a car wildly swaying around the curve toward him.

As the two cars narrowly missed, the driver of the other car shouted at him: "Pig!" He was angry as he drove on around the curve—till he saw, in the middle of the road ahead, a huge pig.)

For some people, this dramatic shift in understanding comes when a family member or good friend comes out of the closet. For others, it's a slow series of little aha's.

These little epiphanies may range from our first meeting with a homosexual person who doesn't fit the stereotype (singer Holly Near, for example, who was a Miss America finalist) to realizing that what broke up a long-term same-sex relationship were many of the same issues that divide a straight couple.

There's a progression that we all seem to go through as "recovering homophobics"—and we don't always make it through the four steps:

Distaste. This is the "norm," the revulsion we grew up with. To me there's something abnormal about the man—it's usually a man—who beats his breast and angrily proclaims, "I'm tired of being called homophobic! How dare they!"

Properly nurtured, this repugnance can translate into seeing gay people as the sign of the downfall of the church, the whole country, or of Western civilization as we know it.

Tolerance. We may feel a twinge of guilt at telling a "limp-wrist" story, and would never use *faggot.* We are aware of a few gay or lesbian acquaintances, and don't object as long as they don't "flaunt" it.

Acceptance. We converse with lesbians, gay men, and bisexuals at work or in social settings. We welcome them at church, but may worry that too many might show up. Our acceptance is rational, intellectual, but our feelings hold us back.

Affirmation. We welcome gay people as individuals, as unique as the rest of us are, each with special gifts. We don't hesitate to speak of gay friends in conversations with straight people, even (gasp!) in Sunday school. We celebrate the gifts these friends bring to life, as we celebrate our non-gay friends. We may have close friends among them. We welcome them in our pews and in our homes as we do any friend, and consider their sexual nature no more relevant than that of any other friend. We see the way they are continually limited and disvalued by government and other institutions, and work to make ours a more just society.

The struggle is worth it. In the end, the success of our mission as Christians will not be measured by how well we have constructed barriers to keep the "wrong" people out, but rather by how we reflected Christ's love.

Like the early Christians, deeply divided over the question of whether uncircumcized gentiles should be welcomed in the church, we can come through to the day when

> there is no longer Jew or Greek, there is no longer slave or free, there is no longer male and female; for all of you are one in Christ Jesus. And if you belong to Christ, then you are Abraham's offspring, heirs according to the promise.
>
> *—Galatians 3:28, 29*

119

If you love Jesus, work for justice. Anybody can honk.

—*Bumper sticker*

Bibliography

Suggestions for Further Reading

Alexander, Scott W., ed. *The Welcoming Congregation*. Boston: The Unitarian Universalist Association, 1990. Useful workbook, workshop ideas, and readings for a congregation seeking to be more open to gay, lesbian, and bisexual people.

Blumenfield, Warren J. and Raymond, Diane. *Looking at Gay and Lesbian Life*. Boston: Beacon Press, 1988.

Borhek, Mary V. *My Son Eric: A Mother Struggles to Accept Her Gay Son and Discover Herself*. New York: Pilgrim Press, 1979.

————. *Coming Out to Parents: A Two-Way Survival Guide for Lesbians and Gay Men and Their Parents*. New York: Pilgrim Press, 1983. Good insights for any reader.

Boswell, John E. *Christianity, Social Tolerance, and Homosexuality*. Chicago: University of Chicago Press, 1980. Winner of the 1981 American Book

Award for History. Fascinating and revealing study of the rise of homophobia in the late Middle Ages.

Bozett, Frederick W. *Homosexuality and the Family.* New York: Harrington Park Press, 1986.

Clark, Don. *Loving Someone Gay.* Berkeley, Calif.: Celestial Arts, 1987. "For gay people and the friends, families, and therapists who want to understand and support them."

Cook, Ann Thompson. *And God Loves Each One.* Useful study booklet beautifully produced by Dumbarton UMC, Washington, D.C. Available from the Reconciling Congregation Program, P.O. Box 23636, Washington, D.C. 20026.

Denman, Rose Mary. *Let My People In.* New York: William Morrow, 1990. Former UMC pastor's story of her coming out and widely discussed church trial.

Fairchild, Betty and Hayward, Nancy. *Now That You Know: What Every Parent Should Know About Homosexuality.* Harcourt Brace Jovanovich, 1979.

Fortunato, John. *Embracing the Exile: Healing Journeys of Gay Christians.* San Francisco: Harper & Row, 1988.

Furnish, Victor Paul. *The Moral Teaching of Paul,* rev. ed. Nashville: Abingdon Press, 1985. Chapter on homosexuality gives solid insight into Paul's troublesome passages.

Glaser, Chris. *Coming Out to God.* Louisville: Westminster/John Knox Press, 1991. Sixty prayers; devotional literature without homophobia.

Grahn, Judy. *Another Mother Tongue.* Boston: Beacon Press, 1984. History and tradition of the gay culture, richly told.

Heger, Heinz. *The Men with the Pink Triangle.* Boston: Alyson Publications, 1980. Moving true story of a gay German man sent to a concentration camp because of his orientation.

Herdt, Gilbert, ed. *Gay and Lesbian Youth.* New York: Harrington Park Press, 1989. Teenagers' struggles in various cultures.

Heron, Ann, ed. *One Teenager in Ten: Writings by Gay and Lesbian Youth.* Boston: Alyson Publications, 1983.

Heyward, Carter. *Our Passion for Justice: Images of Power, Sexuality, and Liberation.* New York: Pilgrim Press, 1984.

Hilton, Bruce. *First Do No Harm: Wrestling with the New Medicine's Life-and-Death Decisions.* Nashville: Abingdon Press, 1991.

McNeill, John H. *The Church and the Homosexual.* Boston: Beacon Press, 1988. A positive message for Roman Catholic lesbians and gay men.

Meyers, Patricia Ann. *Here Is My Hand.* Oregon-Idaho Conference, The United Methodist Church. A five-session study for church groups, leading to consideration of whether to become a Reconciling Congregation. Available from the Reconciling Congregation Program, P.O. Box 23636, Washington, D.C. 20026.

Mollenkott, Virginia and Scanzoni, Letha. *Is the Homosexual My Neighbor? Another Christian View.* San Francisco: Harper & Row, 1978. Mollenkott is an evangelical Bible scholar with an accepting approach to homosexual people.

Mickey, Paul. *Of Sacred Worth.* Nashville: Abingdon Press, 1991. A compassionate but traditional discussion of gay men and lesbians in the church, defending the view that monogamous, long-term marriage is the only setting in which God's hope for human sexuality can be fulfilled.

Nelson, James B. *Between Two Gardens: Reflections on Sexuality and Religious Experience.* New York: Pilgrim Press, 1983.

————. *Embodiment: An Approach to Sexuality and Christian Theology.* Augsburg Publishing House, 1978. Readable theology; insights that do not go out of date.

————. *The Intimate Connection.* Philadelphia: Westminster Press, 1988. A book about "whole men," who have begun to question traditionally held roles and values.

Open Hands. Journal of the Reconciling Congregation Program, P.O. Box 23636, Washington, D.C. 20026. Beautifully designed, thoughtfully edited, twenty-four-page quarterly magazine.

Osterman, Mary Jo. *Homophobia Is a Social Disease.* Evanston, Ill.: Kinheart, 1987.

Parr, Suzanne. *Homophobia: A Weapon of Sexism.* Little Rock: Women's Project, 1988. Available from Women's Project, 222 Main Street, Little Rock, AR 72206.

Report of the Committee to Study Homosexuality. Dayton: General Council on Ministries, The United Methodist Church, 1991. Historic document; can be used for study groups. Available from GCOM, 601 West Riverview, Dayton, OH 45406.

Scroggs, Robin. *The New Testament on Homosexuality: Contextual Background for Contemporary Debate.* Minneapolis: Fortress Press, 1983.

Weber, Joseph C. "What the Bible Seems to Say . . . But Does It?" *Engage/Social Action* (June 1975).

Help and Information

Support Groups and Programs

Affirmation: United Methodists for Lesbian, Gay, and Bisexual Concerns

P.O. Box 1021
Evanston, IL 60201
The support group and activist caucus of gay United Methodist people and their friends.

Parents and Friends of Lesbians and Gays (Parents-FLAG or P-FLAG)

Information and support through many local chapters. A warm, dedicated group of people who have been through many trials. A life-saver for families. Call 202-638-4200 for further information.

Reconciling Congregations Program

3801 N. Keeler Ave.
Chicago, IL 60641
Assists United Methodist congregations in the study of the issues in a declaration—if they should choose to

make one—of openness at all levels to lesbians, gay men, and bisexuals. More than fifty churches across the denomination have chosen to make such a declaration.

Evangelicals Concerned
311 East Seventy-second Street
No. G-1
New York, NY 10021
212-517-3171
A concerned and affirming task force founded by the National Association of Evangelicals.

Kinheart
Conducts workshops across the country at your invitation on homophobia and issues of sexual justice. Much experience and success. For more information call 312-491-1103.

* * *

Videotapes

Casting Out Fear: Reconciling Ministries with Gay/Lesbian United Methodists. 38 minutes. The human story of the struggles of lesbian and gay church members and the churches that try to be truly open to all. Write to Reconciling Congregation Program, P.O. Box 23636, Washington, D.C. 20026; $50 to purchase, $20 to rent.

Listening, Learning, and Loving. 30 miinutes. Detroit Parents-FLAG. Write to Elinor Lewallen, 2258 Kranmeria Street, Denver, CO 80207.